Buck Simmons
The Living Legend

by
Gary L. Parker

WALDENHOUSE PUBLISHERS, INC.
WALDEN, TENNESSEE

Buck Simmons: The Living Legend
Copyright 2017© Gary L. Parker. All rights reserved. No part of this book may be reproduced in any form or by any electronic or mechanical means including information storage and retrieval systems, without permission in writing from the author. The only exception is by a reviewer, who may quote short excerpts in a review.
Cover photo of Buck Simmons courtesy of David Allio
Cover, type and design by Karen Paul Stone
Published by Waldenhouse Publishers, Inc.
100 Clegg Street, Signal Mountain, Tennessee 37377 USA
888-222-8228   www.waldenhouse.com
Printed in the United States of America
ISBN: 978-1-935186-90-8
Library of Congress Control Number: 2017903833

 Career of Baldwin, Georgia's, Charles Leroy "Buck" Simmons. "The Living Legend" of dirt racing, he drove jalopies, modifieds, skeeters, and dirt late models against some of the best drivers in the nation. Simmons scored 1,012 career wins and is in the National Dirt Late Model Hall of Fame. 100 photographs. -- Provided by publisher

 SPO028000 Sports & Recreation - Motor Sports
 SPO019000 Sports & Recreation - History
 TRA001050 Transportation: Automotive - History
 HIS036120 History: United States - South

Other books by this author:

Red Clay and Dust: The Evolution of Southern Dirt Racing
Copyright 2015© Gary L. Parker ISBN: 978-1-935186-61-8
Library of Congress Control Number: 2015911265

The Rock-em, Sock-em, Travelin' Sideways Dirt Show:
A History of Robert Smawley's NDRA
Copyright © 2016 Gary L. Parker. ISBN: 978-1-935186-69-4
Library of Congress Control Number: 2016900468

Herb "Tootle" Estes: The Little Engine That Could
Copyright © 2016 Gary L. Parker. ISBN: 978-1-935186-82-3
Library of Congress Control Number 2016915147

To order contact the author, Gary L. Parker
1517 Maxwell Road, Chattanooga, TN 37412
423-580-2690 • eparker0923@gmail.com

    or go to
www. waldenhouse.com – or –www.amazon.com

DEDICATION

To my friend Tim Simmons.

Tim pointed me in the right direction on a lot of material, photos, and stories on Buck Simmons. He also introduced me to a number of people who had some valuable insights into Buck's life, before and during his racing career. Tim was the key player in making this book a reality. I hope you enjoy BUCK SIMMONS: "The Living Legend" as much as I enjoyed writing it.

Buck Simmons

TABLE OF CONTENTS

DEDICATION	iii
FOREWORD BY BARRY WRIGHT	vii
ACKNOWLEDGMENTS	xi
INTRODUCTION	xiii
BUCK'S FAMILY	xv
Chapter One: THE MODIFIED AND SKEETER YEARS	16
Chapter Two: EARLY LATE MODEL CAREER	27
Chapter Three: THE RISE OF THE NDRA	40
Chapter Four: BUCK'S NDRA YEARS THRU 1981	46
Chapter Five: BUCK'S NDRA YEARS 1982 TO 1985	65
Chapter Six: THE BARRY WRIGHT YEARS	77
Chapter Seven: RACING CLOSER TO HOME	92
Chapter Eight: THE SIMMONS/VOYLES RACE TEAM: THE CHASE FOR 1000 WINS	98
Chapter Nine: BUCK'S TWO FAVORITE WINS	106
Chapter Ten: SOME FINAL THOUGHTS ON THE LIVING LEGEND	113
BACK OF THE BOOK PHOTOS	120
ABOUT THE AUTHOR	128
ORDER BLANK	129

Buck Simmons

Gary Parker

FOREWORD

Charles Leroy Simmons, best known as Buck, was definitely a "living legend." This was his nickname for as long as I can remember. Buck was a true racer at heart. He could compensate for an ill handling car all on his own. He was blessed with the talent to drive and Buck had dirt track racing in his blood. It was his livelihood, and he loved it.

Back in the early years of my racing career, the early 1970's, we started hearing about the "fast drivers from Georgia." We were racing locally at Gaffney, South Carolina, and Shelby, North Carolina. We sure hoped those "fast drivers" wouldn't come to South or North Carolina to race against us, but it was inevitable. They came and invaded us! And true to the rumor mill, they were fast!

I first met Buck in 1975 at Cherokee Speedway in Gaffney, South Carolina. He was one of the "fast drivers from Georgia" that I mentioned earlier. He was driving for someone else at that time. I had watched him race a few times and noticed his driving skills. We became fast friends.

Fortune came my way when Buck became my "house Car" driver from 1982-1987 and then again from 1990-1992. The very first weekend we raced, we won all 4 races we ran. That Thursday night, we raced at Sugar Creek Speedway in Union, South Carolina. Buck started on the pole and led every lap to win $5000. Remember, this was our first time racing together, and we just clicked. Next was NDRA racing at Portsmouth, Ohio, where we set fast time and won the $10,000 winner's share of the purse. Saturday night we were in Chillicothe, Ohio, for another NDRA race. We again started on the pole, and except for a few laps, led all the race, and Buck took the win. Chalk up another $10,000. And to think, these purses were paid out in 1982! Next on the agenda, we stopped at Tazewell, Tennessee, on our way home that Sunday. Buck again started on the pole and led all but the first 2 laps for the win.

Perhaps one of the most memorable wins was the NDRA Invitational race in Kingsport, Tennessee, in 1985. I will never forget the feeling of winning the pole at Kingsport, Tennessee – that paid a cool $10,000. Then, Buck led every lap of the race to take the win for another $20,000. What an unforgettable weekend that was! The money was great, don't get me wrong, but the fact that we won the pole and then led every lap for the win – well that was the icing on the cake. We had built a car just for this race, not a wedge car like we were used to running, but a more "stock" looking car. He handled it just as well as he had been handling the wedge cars.

As a team with Buck, I think we won about 200 races together. Buck had more than 1,000 wins at the time of his death. That is quite an accomplishment in any racer's book. With that many wins, he was put in an elite status. I doubt many drivers can say they have won 1,000 times. At one point in those years with me, Buck won an astonishing 18 races in a row. He was a tremendous, talented driver who took care of the equipment.

Buck had the ability to put the car in the turns as smoothly as anyone could. He had a way of knowing how to adjust the car to the situation, even if the setup wasn't exactly what it should be. In a lap or two, he would have made that adjustment and made it look easy. He never complained about the car, and would take care of the car better than most. It was uncanny how he truly almost never wrecked the car. If he did happen to get into trouble on the track, he would apologize for damaging the car.

He couldn't always tell me what the car was doing, so I really had to watch him to "see" what it was doing. Along with his ability to drive around the problem, watching him for adjustments on my end made me a better racer.

Perhaps one of Buck's greatest racing skills was being an excellent qualifier. This gave him a great advantage. He had an eye for finishing races and mostly stayed out of trouble on the track. He was smooth for sure, always keeping his eye on the front and setting himself up to get there – if he wasn't already there. He was also a clean driver, racing furiously side-by-side with others and rarely ever getting into another race car.

Buck, Kevin Brown and I had some great years racing together. I feel fortunate to have worked with Buck as long as I did. Together, we became better racers. He is a friend that I truly miss and I'm so thankful I got to work with him. He should be remembered as one of the best ever on a dirt track

Barry Wright
Barry Wright Race Cars, Inc.
2002 National Dirt Late Model Hall of Fame

Buck Simmons

Gary Parker

ACKNOWLEDGMENTS

It is now one of my favorite times of writing a book. Giving credit to the people who played a major role in making this book a reality.

The person I probably owe the most credit to is Buck's cousin, Tim Simmons. Tim was able to point me to people, places, and information that I probably would not otherwise have found on my own. He also provided some personal photos for the book.

Specials thanks go to my friend and National Dirt Hall of Fame chassis builder, Barry Wright. Thanks, Barry, for a great foreword to this book.

At this time I want to thank Karen and Charlie Stone at Waldenhouse Publishers for the great work they have done on all of my books on dirt late model racing.

I also want to thank the many photographers for the great photos they provided. Among those were Gene Lefler, Tony Hammett, David Allio, and others whose names appear in the captions. A very special thanks is in order to David Allio for the use of his photo of Buck Simmons that is the cover for this book. A truly great photo of Simmons.

Others who played a part in this book include my friend and fellow racing historian, Bob Markos. I can always count on him for any articles and photos I am in need of. I just e-mail him and within a couple of days he sends what I need with a "Here ya go Gary" at the end.

Many others I owe thanks to also. They include Gerald Voyles, the last car owner Simmons drove for. It was in Voyles'

John Deere green #41 that Buck scored his win number 1000. Gerald also provided valuable information and personal photos for the book.

Others who played a role in the book include Harold "Speedy" Evans, J.R. Whitt, Leon Sells, Bud Lunsford, Wayne Wells, the Buck Simmons family, the Max Simpson family, Billy Thomas, and many others.

A final thanks is in order to anyone I may have overlooked, thank you also.

In closing, I want to thank all my readers and the race fans. It is for you and the sport of dirt late model racing that I continue to write about the sport that I love.

Gary L. Parker

Gary Parker

INTRODUCTION

BUCK SIMMONS: "The Living Legend" tells the story of Charles Leroy Simmons. At an early age Simmons knew his place in the world would be behind the wheel of a race car.

As a teenager he started racing when most teens were thinking about summer break. In the early 1960's He began racing and winning in jalopies; he then moved to modifieds, super modifieds, and on to the ultra fast Skeeters.

By the time he entered the popular dirt late model ranks in the mid-'60's he had already scored a lot more wins than most of the older dirt stars he was competing against. His raw natural driving ability was clearly brought to light in the late '60's and early '70's at a new track in Woodstock, Georgia known as Dixie Speedway. In the beginning, he almost dominated the track, winning 18 of the 22 races in 1969.

Later, he would win the 1978 National 100 at East Alabama Motor Speedway, catching the eye of track owner, Jimmy Thomas. Thomas hired Simmons to drive one of his new Jig-A-Lo chassis race cars. He wanted a veteran driver to team with his young sons, Billy and Bobby, to help with their racing careers, and to help promote his new racing chassis.

Buck seemed always to be at the right place at the right time. In 1978 a rebel racing promoter by the name of Robert Smawley introduced the dirt racing world to his new national series known as the NDRA. Simmons would go on to drive in the NDRA series for Jimmy Thomas, Darrell Monk, Jim Erp, Barry Wright, and others. He would carve his place in NDRA history, winning the 1981 series title and going on to become the NDRA all time wins leader with 23 checkered flags.

Simmons then teamed with Cowpens, South Carolina, race car builder, Barry Wright, from 1982 until the early '90's. They proved to be a potent pair, scoring almost 200 victories in late models, and wedge outlaw race cars.

After brief driving stints with Wade Hegler and Morris Partain, Buck had decided that with almost a thousand wins he had nothing left to prove on the national dirt scene and returned to his Baldwin, Georgia home.

Then in the late '90's, Shane Worley convinced Simmons to drive locally in the Northeast Georgia area and try and reach that elusive 1000th victory. Over the next few years Buck drove for Worley, Gerald Voyles, Bruce Taylor, Tim Simmons, and Slab Sellers.

In the end, it was with Gerald Voyes and the John Deere green #41 that he scored that 1000th win at Lavonia (GA) Speedway on May 11, 2002. He would go on to record 1,012 wins during his National Dirt Late Model Hall of Fame career. In the end, I believe he was the best driver to ever strap into a dirt late model race race-car. He truly was, BUCK SIMMONS: "The Living Legend."

CHARLES LEROY "BUCK" SIMMONS FAMILY

Charles Leroy "Buck" Simmons

Place of birth: Clarksville, GA
Born: July 31, 1946
Died: August 12, 2012

Father: Amos Simmons   Mother: Faye House Simmons

Sisters: Wanda Simmons Garrison, Irma Simmons Herrin

Children: Stepson, Brock Johnson; Son, Colt Simmons

Daughters: Stormie Simmons, Cassidy Simmons, and Starleigh Simmons

Wife: Tracee Allen Simmons

Buck's parents, Amos and Faye Simmons

Chapter One
THE MODIFIED AND SKEETER YEARS

The dirt racing world will always associate Buck Simmons with the legendary career he enjoyed in dirt late models. In a career than spanned over five decades, Simmons would go on to be, in my opinion, the best dirt late model driver to ever strap into a race car. Buck had what only a very few in the dirt racing world will ever possess, he had raw natural talent.

Taking a look back now, Buck started his racing career when most kids his age were still in high school and looking forward to summer break. According to Georgia Racing Hall of Famer Tommy Irvin, who owned the Banks County Speedway at the time, "Buck started hanging out at the track when he was around 12 years old." Irvin continued, "One day Buck came up and asked if he could drive the water truck. After giving it some thought I asked his dad, Amos, if it would be alright and he said yes." Tommy went on to say, "Buck did this on Saturdays for a while. Then, not long after that he got an old car and started driving around on the track while we worked." In closing Irvin said, "Finally Amos put him in his first race car when he was 14 years old. So at that young age, it was at my Banks County Speedway were it all began." Some people have told me Buck's first race car was a 1951 Oldsmobile that he first raced at Toccoa (GA) Speedway.

It didn't take the teenager long to record his first win. That win occurred at a speedway in Westminister, South

Carolina, in only his fifth (some sources have said his third race) career start. And so began the legendary racing career of Charles Leroy "Buck" Simmons.

It was during the mid-60's that a kid, known to the dirt racing world as Buck Simmons, would begin his march toward becoming a dirt racing legend. Early on, Simmons ran a lot of sportsman (early late models) events during the mid-60's at tracks that included the Athens (GA) Speedway, and the Banks County (GA) Speedway. Another track where he scored a number of early sportsman wins was the Greenville (SC) Fairgrounds Speedway. At one point the young teenager won two races in a row there in what the track began calling the "Wild Hog" division because of all the wild racing action that included a lot of wrecks and roll overs.

A young Buck Simmons standing beside his #41 super modified skeeter. (Photo from the Georgia Racing Hall of Fame and Gerald Voyles.)

However, it was in the modifieds, super modifieds (fuel injected, with straight drive transmissions) and "skeeters" (super modifieds with a wing on top) that the young mud-slinger would begin to make a name for himself. The young teenager competed night after night with some of the giants of the sport at the time. Drivers like, Tootle Estes, Bud Lunsford, Charlie Padgett, Cabbage Pendley, Bill York, Charlie Mincey, T.C. Hunt, Harold and Freddy Fryar, Doug Kenimer, Charlie Burkhalter, and many others.

While driving James "Jabo" Bradberry's modified 1932 Ford coupe, powered by a 327ci Chevy engine, Buck began scoring victories over many of the drivers mentioned above at tracks all over the Southeast. Some of those tracks included, the Cherokee Speedway in Gaffney, South Carolina; a track known as "The Mountain" in Cumming, Georgia; the Athens (GA) Speedway; the Banks County Speedway near Homer, Georgia; the Anderson (SC) Speedway; and even a few trips to the Peach Bowl in Atlanta, Georgia, to name but a few.

Two of the most unique modified wins of his early career occurred on a Labor Day weekend at a track in Tennessee known as the Kingsport Speedway. It was two 50 lap modified races. The winner of the first race would have to start last in the second race. Buck won the first 50 lap event. The field was reversed for the second race. However, this didn't stop the lead-footed Simmons from racing through the entire field to claim both of the holiday races. As you will see later, this was a feat he would accomplish several more times during his career.

In another memorable win that occurred before the largest ever crowd at Anderson (SC) Speedway. The Speedway had scheduled a special 100 lap modified championship race on a Monday night for what it called the "Bud Lunsford

Night." Lunsford was being honored for his past track accomplishments, that included 37 feature wins. That night Track promoter Charlie Mize presented Lunsford with a picture of Bud standing by the car that he won 19 features in the year before. However, a young driver from Baldwin, Georgia was about to steal the night's thunder. Buck Simmons took the early lead and held on for the big win. Bud Lunsford, the night's spotlight driver, chased Simmons to the finish line, finishing on the young upstarts rear bumper.

In a recent phone conversation with racing legend Bud Lunsford, he said of Simmons, "He was probably the most talented kid at his age in a race car that I had ever seen. The only one that I can think of that had talent close to that was a young Doug Kenimer when he was in his late teens and early twenties."

In 1963 the 17 year old Simmons began racing in the skeeter division at Cherokee Speedway in Gaffney, SC. Buck had been racing in the modified division at the track; but decided to step up to the winged skeeters that were rapidly gaining in popularity in Georgia, South Carolina, and even into Tennessee.

During the early 1960's Cherokee Speedway was only a 1/4-mile dirt track (only later would it would go to a half-mile). At one point, while running the skeeters, the young 17 year old Simmons reeled of five consecutive wins at Cherokee against some of the best competition in the South at the time. His winning streak was finally broken by another Georgian, Marvin Moore of Eberton, Georgia in a 1932 Ford skeeter.

A number of his skeeter wins were recorded at, Banks County Speedway, The Mountain, and several other tracks in South Carolina and Georgia. Bud Lunsford, Charlie Mincey, Doug Kenimer, Cabbage Pendley, Charley Burkhalter, and

Charlie Padgett were among the many dirt stars that the teenager was able to score victories over in the increasingly popular skeeters ranks.

Buck Simmons takes the checkered flag at "The Mountain" Speedway in Cumming, Georgia (Photo provided by J.R. Whitt.)

Buck would continue to race skeeters through the late '60's for car builders like, the above mentioned, James "Jabo," Bradberry. One of the last skeeters Buck drove was the gold #41 of Harold "Speedy" Evans and J.R. Whitt. Their race car was the one to beat at a nearby Cumming, Georgia speedway known as The Mountain.

The dawn of the 1970's saw a "New Kid" on the block introduced to the dirt racing world. The old "sportsman" class would become the "late model" division. Dirt late models would become the future of dirt racing. The popularity of this division was simple; the race cars looked like cars the race fans were driving. Early on, the 1955-56 Fords and Chevys were the cars of choice in dirt late model racing. Later, those race cars gave way the 1964-67 Chevy Chevelles, and the Ford Fairlanes. Finally, the Chevy Camaro, the Pontiac Firebird, and the Ford Mustangs were the cars of choice as the dawn of the 1980's began.

As we go through Buck's career in the dirt late model ranks we will continue to see the evolution of the dirt late model, from the first "home built" race cars to the 850hp "super" dirt late models of today. After this brief look at his early career the stage is now set for the main focus of this book, the dirt late model racing career of Buck Simmons.

Simmons powers thru turns three and four at "The Mountain" Speedway (Photo provided by J.R. Whitt.)

Simmons and Doug Kemmer #42 doing battle at "The Mountain" Speedway (Photo provided by J.R. Whitt.)

Moore Finishes Third

Simmons Repeats As 'Wild Hogs' Tangle

The season's largest racing crowd, estimated at better than 1,000, should have gotten their money's worth last night at the Greenwood Fairgrounds Speedway before little Buck Simmons, Athens, Ga. became the first repeat winner here in the sportsman 35-lap main event.

If they came to see spills, flipovers and some hard fender-bumping racing they shouldn't have been disappointed.

The "wild hogs", as they are sometimes called in amateur racing, were so hungry for first money in the 35-lap main event that four of the starting 16 cars were eliminated before the first lap could officially be completed. It took nearly 30 minutes to get the feature sportsman cars rolling in high gear but they still finished the program in two hours and 15 minutes.

Carl Hall, driving a Blue coach, No. 5, took the worst spill as he flipped over on his top in the first turn but came away without injury.

Westminster's Marvin Moore, winner of the season's opener here, turned in the night's best performance as he started in the rear but finished strong in third place just behind Floyd Holcombe, who was pushing Simmons for the lead spot several times.

Charlie Bryant and Ross Marcengill took fourth and fifth place money in the sportsman main event.

Simmons and L. D. Mauldin, Salem, driving an orange coupe, No. 21, won the heat events in the sportsman division. Mauldin proved a surprise threat, beating off challenges by Bryant and Aaron Gailey, who was driving the No. 2 car, owned by Jim Hall of Anderson.

Moore, ending up on his top in the third turn after going too wide in the second heat, appeared he was finished for the night but quickly got his car ready in time to catch the main event starting field on the backstretch in the rear starting position.

Tommy Bullard, Greenwood, and George Marion, another of the new drivers coming here, wrecked on the final lap of the first heat, Marion winding up on his side. Both escaped without injury. J. T. Foster, Greenville. and Marcengill were other sportsman drivers having their troubles in the heat races.

Greenwood's Olin Kirkland took the hobby division feature, beating out Earl Johnson, also of Greenwood. Jerry Hilley, Greenwood, defending champion who has yet to win, tangled with L. J. Honea on the first lap in front of the main grandstand.

Simmons Victim Of 'Oldest Law'

GAFFNEY, S. C. — The law of averages caught up with 17-year-old Buck Simmons at Cherokee Speedway last Saturday night. The leadfooted youngster, who had posted five consecutive wins at the 1/4-mile dirt track, was ousted from his track supremacy in the super-modified division by Marvin Moore of Eberton, Ga., who drove a 1932 Ford to victory in the 40-lap main event race.

Simmons had five straight wins in as many weeks but ran into some faster cars and had to settle for a fifth place finish.

Tommy Eskew of Shelby was the big winner in the 25-lap semi-modified feature while Red Doggett of Caroleen and Carl Falls of Kings Mountain gained victories in the two 10-lap heat races.

PEACH HOSTS 'SKEETERS'

The fastest set of Atlanta chauffeurs in years, drivers of the "305" skeeters, gather for a 30-lap feature Friday night at the Peach Bowl. Led by Charley Mincey, who won last week's feature, the field will include the ever-popular Bud Lunsford, Charley Padgett, Red Cruce, Bob Leach, Charley Burkhalter and the new sensation, Buck Simmons.

Simmons, only 19, is the hottest young driver to hit the Atlanta scene in several seasons— a proving grounds in the past for such drivers as Bobby Johns and the late Fireball Roberts — he was leading the last skeeter show, but spun out five laps before the finish and wound up second.

In addition to the skeeter race there will be a jalopy run of 25 laps, with heat races and a consolation in both divisions. Gates open at 7:30 p.m. for practice, with the races following.—ROBINSON.

TOMORROW NIGHT
Another Close Battle Is Expected At Local Track

BUCK SIMMONS

Doug Kenimer, a 20-year-old race car driver from Dahlonega, Ga., driving a newly built engine, will return to Anderson Speedway here tomorrow night and attempt to break Buck Simmons' winning streak of two-straight races.

Simmons, of Baldwin, Ga., who recently turned 20, fought a terrific battle to win the last two feature events here and is expected to have another hard time tomorrow night.

Two more drivers expected to push Simmons to the finish line are Aaron Gailey and Steve Chastain, both from Lavonia, Ga. Gailey will be driving a car with a new engine in the 35-lap race.

Another possible winner is Wilton Watkins of Baldwin, Ga., a brother-in-law of Simmons, who has been finishing in the top three driving Jim Bradshaw's car.

Last Friday 18 cars lined up for the feature with only eight finishing after a mass of wrecks that sent Jim Hall of Anderson to the hospital.

Six events are scheduled for tomorrow night's show which gets underway at 8 p.m.

Buck Simmons *Wins 2 Races*

Buck Simmons of Athens, Ga., won two 50-lap modified races at Kingsport Speedway Saturday night as the track held its annual Labor Day weekend events.

Simmons was ahead at the end of the first 50 laps. The field was then reversed, putting the front cars to the back, but he leadfooted his way back into the lead.

Winner of the 40-lap amateur race was Fred Clevenger of Kingsport.

RACING ROUNDUP

WESTMINSTER SPEEDWAY — Saturday night's winners: Amateur heats — Sam Kelly and Sam Dickson. Sportsman heats — Marvin Moore and Tommy Roberts. Jalopy events L. J. Honea, Dawson Alexander, and Sam Owens. Amateur main — 1. Sam Dickson, 2 — Floyd Holcomb, 3 — Benny Evatt. Sportsman main — 1 — Buck Simmons, 2 — Marvin Moore, 3. — Floyd Holcomb.

BUD LUNSFORD, Gainesville, Ga., driver, shown with his wife Liquetta and four-year-old daughter Debbie, was honored Monday night at Anderson Speedway. (Independent Sports Photo by Jack Cromer)

Lunsford Night Attracts Big Crowd; Simmons Wins

Buck Simmons, Baldwin, Ga., won the 100-lap modified championship race at the Anderson Speedway Monday night before the largest crowd ever to attend a modified race at the local oval.

Bud Lunsford, honored by the speedway for his sportsmanship and driving ability, finished on the bumper of Simmons' car.

Friday night is "Bonus Night" for area racing fans, the bonus in the form of a double feature race for the regular admission. A 50-lap sportsman feature and a 50-lap late model feature and scheduled for the program which includes the jalopies for a 15-lap event. Race-time is 8 p. m.

Lunsford had led the race until the 72nd lap after having taken the lead from Simmons on the 21st lap. Aaron Gailey, Lavonia, Ga., driving his modified No. 50, did a beautiful job of handling his racer when the accelerator hung wide open as he went into the No. 3 corner on the 13th lap of the feature, which he was leading, after having taken that lead on the first lap.

Steve Chastain, five-time winner of the weekly sportsman races, finished third.

Promoter Charlie Mize had proclaimed Monday as Bud Lunsford night. Lunsford was presented the green and checkered flags under which he had won 37 features at the track. Lunsford has won over 400 races during his 12-year racing career. On the green flag was monogramed "A Grand Guy and a Great Sportsman." Monogramed on the checkered flag: "37 Wins — Anderson Speedway 1963-66. Also presented to Lunsford was a huge picture of Lunsford standing alongside the car in which he won 19 features in 1963. Lettered on the picture in 23 karet gold: "Champion of Champions."

Gailey won the modified heat, Chastain the sportsman heat. Charles Owens took the jalopy main followed by Charles Robinson. Jim Brown and Robinson were jalopy heat winners.

Gary Parker

Chapter Two
EARLY LATE MODEL CAREER

As the 1960's were fading into the sunset, a young Baldwin, Georgia driver by the name of Buck Simmons was about to begin his journey into dirt late model racing immortality. Already a seasoned veteran in dirt racing by the time he reached his 20th birthday, Buck began his late model career in the late '60's. Two of the first people Simmons drove dirt late models for was the team of Harold "Speedy" Evans and J.R Whitt out of a Cumming, Georgia garage. According to J.R., "Speedy and I worked well together. I did most of the chassis and body work and Speedy did what he did best, tune the engines." Whitt closed by saying, "We had a good

A view of one of the big crowds that were always at the Hartwell (GA) Speedway for the Saturday night races in the late 1960's and early '70's. (Photo provided by J.R. Whitt.)

thing going at the time, especially with the young driver we had, Buck Simmons. He had already proved his ability to us with our skeeter car that he had been driving."

The late '60's saw Simmons begin to dominate at several dirt tracks in the region. He was one of the drivers to beat at the nearby Hartwell Speedway. At the time, Hartwell was one of the tracks in the area that ran the aluminum wings atop the late models. It was there where a number of classic battles between Simmons, in his black and gold #41 Chevelle, and Colbert, Georgia's Rudy Burroughs, in his #007 "Swamp Guinea" 1964 Chevelle took place.

Rudy Burroughs in the "Swamp Guinea" #007. The Swamp Guinea Restaruant's slogan was, "Come pick a bone with us." (Photo from the 1969 Hartwell Speedway racing program.)

It was during the 1968 season that Buck and another Georgia driver, Charlie Mincey, would briefly swap rides. Mincey was driving a 1955 Chevy #77 for Powder Springs, Georgia's Ed Massey and Buck was driving the Speedy Evans #41 Chevelle. The two went head to head in ten races with Mincey winning the battle, taking eight of the 10 races over Simmons in just a short period of time.

However, it was a new dirt track north of Atlanta that Simmons would begin writing his chapter in dirt late model racing history. It was the Spring of 1969 and Cherokee County businessman, Max Simpson, along with dirt racing star Bud Lunsford had just opened a new track called Dixie Speedway. The 3/8th mile banked red clay oval was located in a tiny town north of Atlanta known as Woodstock, Georgia.

During the track's first few years of racing, some of the most exciting races found in the South were held there every Saturday night. On any given Saturday night the overflow crowd was sometimes treated to as many as dozen late model drivers with a legitimate chance to take the checkered flag. Some of those drivers included Doug Kenimer, Leon Sells, Charlie Mincey, Luther Carter, Leon Archer, Jody Ridley, and of course Buck Simmons.

The opening race of 1969 saw Buck Simmons take the inaugural win at Dixie over a stellar field of cars. He was still driving for J.R. Whitt and Harold "Speedy" Evans. By this time Simmons had started racing dirt late models full time. During first year at this new dirt racing facility, Buck was almost impossible to beat in that black and gold Da-Je Homes/Quality Motor Sales #41. By the end of that '69 season Simmons had scored an amazing 18 wins in the 22 races ran. One of the races was rained out and Mapleton, Georgia's Leon Sells won the other three, driving for his brother-in-law, Ed Massey, in his blue #77 Chevelle.

Simmons continued to be the driver to beat during the 1970 season at Dixie. Although Buck was now traveling more to other tracks, when he raced at Dixie he was still the man to beat. That year saw six different drivers take the Checkered flag. Doug Kenimer won six; Leon Sells and Jody Ridley had three wins each, Charlie Mincey had two victories; while

The DA-JE Homes #41 Speedy Evans Chevelle. This car was driven to a number of wins by Buck Simmons in the late 1960's and early 1970's. (Photo provided by Harold "Speedy" Evans.)

Charlie Padgett found the winner's circle once. However, Simmons continued to dominate the track with 9 trips to victory lane that year.

As mentioned earlier, another car owner Simmons drove briefly for on both the dirt and asphalt tracks was, Ed Massey. He teamed with Leon Sells to compete in identical '64 Chevy Chevelles. In a recent phone conversation with Sells he said, "Buck was a good driver and we had two cars at the time (Charlie Mincey had left the team to take a ride with Day Chevrolet) so we put Buck in the other car. He won a number of races for us at, Senoia, West Atlanta, Newnan, Dixie and places like that."

Looking back now, the year 1973 proved to be a year of change in late model racing. Asphalt tracks in Georgia like the Middle Georgia Raceway outside of Macon; and the half-mile banked track at Jefferson, Georgia; along with asphalt tracks in other areas of the country like Birmingham (AL) International Speedway were doing well.

Max Simpson had gained control of Dixie Speedway at the end of the 1972 season. Now Simpson had decided to roll the dice and pave Dixie. This was an exciting time for racing as a lot of late model drivers started competing on both dirt and asphalt. Buck Simmons, Leon Sells, Charlie Mincey, Doug Kenimer, Jody Ridley and several others scored a number of wins on both during the period. At the time basically all you had to do was change the shocks and tires and you were ready to race on either surface. Leon Sells told me, "Sometimes on Sunday we would run the asphalt track at Macon on Sunday afternoon, then change tires and shocks before we left to race on dirt at Rome on Sunday night."

Around 1973 Simmons would begin driving for Max Simpson. This proved to be a great match for both Buck and Max. Buck won a number of races for Simpson on both dirt and asphalt over the next few years. For example, at Dixie Speedway Simmons had some classic battles with his longtime rival, Jody Ridley. Jody had been winning a number of events at Dixie (Jody would go on to be the all-time asphalt wins leader at Dixie with 46 victories) since it became an asphalt facility. Ridley was so successful driving his '67 Ford Fairlane at Dixie that Max later built one for Buck to drive.

Among Simmons' many victories while driving for Max Simpson was a 400 lap NASCAR sanctioned event at the Minnesota State Fairgrounds Speedway. It was a three day event that took place on August 22-24, 1975. On the first two nights Buck won two preliminary races. On the final night the stage was set to see if Simmons could complete the sweep. Because of the length of the event (400 laps) Simpson had brought Tennessee racing great, L.D. Ottinger to share the driving duties with Simmons. The move proved to be a good one as Simmons and Ottinger went on to take the checkered flag in the big event.

In 1976 Buck added South Alabama Speedway's "Rattler 100" to his trophy case. He finished ahead of two members of famed "Alabama Gang" in that race, beating Donnie Allison, and Red Farmer to the finish line.

Simmons began the 1977 racing season driving for Paul's Auto Parts, located in Soddy-Daisy, Tennessee. Over the years Paul's had a number of great drivers at the wheel of their race cars. Among those were, Tootle Estes, and Charlie Mincey. Now it was Buck's turn to take the wheel of their new "Tiger" Tom Pistone race car. In a recent interview Paul's son, Tommy Hickman said, "Buck drove for us in '77 and I believe a couple of races in '78. A new track had just opened in Tennessee called the Newport Speedway." Tommy recalled, "We went up there for the first race and won. Over the next few months we won the majority of races." Hickman finished by saying, "I believe they finally put a bounty on us and drivers like Doug Kenimer came to try and outrun us. Most of the time at Newport a local driver by the name of Bill Morton was the one we had to beat."

Buck Simmons #41 along side of Doug Kenimer #42 before the start of a race. Buck was driving the Paul's Auto Parts/"Tiger" Tom Pistone race car. (Photo provided by Tommy Hickman.)

Probably the biggest race Simmons won while driving for Paul's was the 1977 "Tiny Lund Memorial" race at the

Summerville (SC) Speedway on August 10th of that year. Tommy Hickman said, "We loaded the car up and headed to South Carolina for the race. At the time I had no idea that it was going to be that big of an event." Hickman continued, "When we got to the pits I looked around and found out there was 202 cars at this race. Well I found Buck and asked him what in the world we were doing there." Tommy then said, "Old Buck said, 'We are here to win this race.' I thought he was crazy til after the long qualifying session was over and there we were on the pole." Hickman closed by saying, "Haskell Willingham started on the outside pole. Well Buck jumped him on the start and took the lead. A short time later, the race was stopped for a big pile up behind them. When the race was restarted Buck led the rest of the race and won."

After this account of the race Tommy said, "The win was not as easy as it sounded. As Buck took the white flag a screw holding the air filter on came off and the stud holding the air filter on fell into the Carburetor." Hickman with a big laugh said, "When he took the checkered flag the engine was

Jimmy Thomas' Jig-A-Lo race team drivers, Billy Thomas, Buck Simmons, and Bobby Thomas. (Photo from the Robert Smawley collection.)

spitting steam and water, if there had been another lap we would not have won that race."

The last part of the 1977 racing season proved to be a good for Simmons. He won the annual "National 100" at East Alabama Motor Speedway in Phenix City, Alabama. By winning that race Buck had caught the eye of track owner Jimmy Thomas. Jimmy, along with his two sons, Billy and Bobby, had just introduced the revolutionary Jig-A-Lo Chassis to the dirt racing world. It was probably the first racing chassis made from nose to tail out of a tubular material. After meeting with Simmons, Thomas decided to add Buck, along with his two sons to his new racing team. Simmons was to act as a mentor to the Thomas brothers in a three car racing team.

A new era was about to begin in dirt late model racing and the Thomas' new Jig-A-Lo chassis would play a key role.

In 1978 a Kingsport, Tennessee businessman, promoter, and showman extraodinaire by the name of Robert Smawley was about to change the face of dirt late model racing forever. Smawley was planning to introduce the dirt racing nation to his new National Dirt Racing Association (NDRA). Through his series he planned to pay unheard of $10,000 to win races, introduce a drivers point championship, and make national racing stars out of regional drivers.

After months of planning Smawley was ready to promote, what he called, his two "test races" held at the nearby Newport (TN) Speedway. The first of these events known as the "Southeastern Classic Dirt Championship" was held on June 9-10, 1978. It was an unheard of $22,000 total purse, 100 lap race with $10,000 going to the winning driver. As far as the "test" went, it was an astounding success. An overflow crowd of excited race fans and a pit full of race cars from all over the country had witnessed Baldwin, Georgia's Buck Sim-

Race cars lined up to get into the Newport (TN) Speedway for the first of Smawley's "test" races in June of 1978. (Photo from the Robert Smawley collection.)

mons take the $10,000 winner's check from Robert Smawley in Victory Lane. Simmons won the race in what else, one of Jimmy Thomas' Jig-A-Lo chassis race cars.

The last of the test races took place in July of '78, with another Georgia driver, Doug Kenimer, taking the checkered flag and the $10,000 share of the $30,000 purse. Both races were more than Smawley could have hoped for. He was now ready to begin his new series and change the face of the sport forever.

Before we go into Smawley's ground breaking NDRA Series in the next few chapters; there is one race that needs to be mentioned here. It was a non-NDRA race that took place in 1979 at the historic one-mile dirt oval known as Lakewood (GA) Speedway, South of Atlanta.

It was the 1979 Labor Day weekend and forty-four cars had come to the famed dirt oval to try and make the field for the "Lakewood Speedway Labor Day 100." With qualifying completed, it was Buford, Georgia's Russell Nelson on the pole, and Buck Simmons starting beside him on the front row.

At the time Simmons was competing on the NDRA trail, driving one of Jimmy Thomas' new Jig-A-Lo chassis race cars. Thomas had brought the #22 Pontiac Firebird for Buck to drive in this big holiday event. As the green flag waved for the start, Simmons jumped to the lead.

From the first lap, it was a torrid battle between Simmons and Nelson for the entire race. In the end, Buck kept Nelson behind him and led the entire 100 laps. I was only fitting that Buck Simmons, a racing legend, would win the last dirt late model race ever held at Lakewood Speedway (See articles below for an account of the race).

Firestone

ROSCOE SMITH RACING EQUIPMENT

The Sweetheart Of Southern Dirt Track Racing
Presents

'The 'Lakewood Speedway Labor Day 100'
For Late Model Modifieds

$3,000 To Win!   **Total Purse - $12,000**
(Plus Contingency Money)

Schedule
Time Trials - *Sunday, Sept. 2 - 1-5 P.M. Sharp!*
Ten-Lap Consolation - *Monday, One P.M.*
(First 5 Finishers Enter 100-Lapper)
'Labor Day 100' - *Monday, Sept. 3*

Feature Payoff

Consi Payoff
1. - $200
2. - $100
3. - $75
4. - $50
5. - $25

Top 3 Qualifiers
Fast Time - $150
Second - $100
Third - $50

Simmons Grabs Lakewood Speedway 100-Miler

ATLANTA, Ga. (Sept. 3) - Starting on the outside front row, Buck Simmons (Baldwin, Ga.) led every lap to win the 100-mile, 100-lap "Lakewood Speedway Labor Day 100" at the Lakewood Fairgrounds Speedway.

Simmons qualified his #22 Pontiac Firebird the day before at 41.60 seconds and sat next to pole-winner Russell Nelson (Buford), who timed in at 41.04 seconds. The entire race was a battle between the two veteran Late Model Sportsman pilots, as they ran neck and neck the entire distance. The race was stopped at the halfway point so the cars could take on fuel and fresh tires, and when the chase resumed, Simmons and Nelson continued their duel around the one-mile clay track.

Simmons took the checkered flag, which was worth $3,000 plus contingency money, in front of Nelson, second, H.W. Tittle, third, Johnny Hunt, fourth and Ronnie Waites, fifth. The top 10 were rounded out by Charlie Bagwell, Lynn Cook, Phillip McElroy, Ronnie Johnson and Dan Scoggins.

Forty-four cars attempted to qualify for the second race this year at the fairgrounds track, but due to mechanical problems and blown engines, only 39 made the starting grid.

Several cars, including that of Sam Sommers, who won the July 29 "Lakewood Sampler", were sidelined by minor accidents or mechanical malfunctions, and the most serious incident of the day occurred when Paul Roberts spun between turns three and four and was hit by another car. He was not injured, but his car was out for the day.

Buck Simmons (left) and Russell Nelson congratulate each other on their respective first and second-place finishes in the "Lakewood Labor Day 100". *Hugh Simpler photo*

The NDLMHoF Corner

BUCK SIMMONS: THE KING OF DIXIE SPEEDWAY

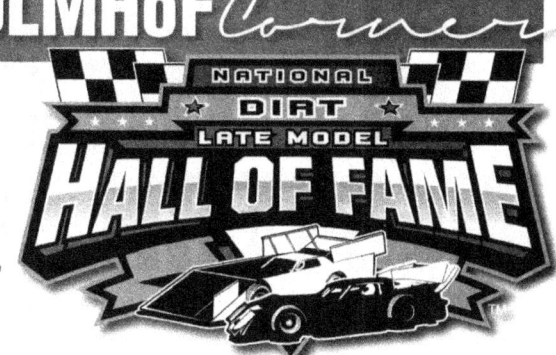

National Dirt Late Model Hall of Fame (2001) driver Buck Simmons was king of a lot of dirt tracks during his long and successful racing career. Perhaps no one was more dominant than Simmons at a new dirt track north of Atlanta in Cherokee County, known as Dixie Speedway, and he was dominant from the very beginning of the track's history.

The year was 1969 and many a Saturday night at Dixie Speedway saw most of the South's best Dirt Late Model drivers show up for a chance at a big win. Southern dirt warriors like Leon Sells, Doug Kenimer, Charlie Mincey, Charlie Padgett and, of course, Buck Simmons. However, it was Simmons in that famous Da-Je Mobile Homes/gold and black #41, Speedy Evans 1964 Chevelle that usually took the checkered flag with one of his many runaway wins that year. That opening season saw Buck cruise to 18 wins out of the scheduled 22 races. According to some sources, one race was rained out; and another future NDLMHOF driver, Leon Sell (2015), won the remaining three races.

Nineteen-seventy saw Simmons traveling to other Southern dirt tracks and continue his winning ways. Among those tracks was yet another new facility at the time, the ultra-fast Atomic (Tennessee) Speedway, along with the one-half mile Cherokee Speedway in Gaffney, South Carolina; and Hartwell (Georgia) Speedway where the race cars were allowed to run aluminum wings on top (see photo). It was during this second year of racing at Dixie that Jody Ridley appeared on the scene. I was a member of Jody's pit crew at the time, and for about a year, we had heard talk of a dominant Atlanta area Dirt Late Model driver by the name of Buck Simmons.

The following story will always remain in my memory about Buck and the early Dixie Speedway days. Simmons, like most of the other drivers at the time, wore "bubble shields" on their helmets. In order to keep the dust out of their nose and mouth, drivers would use a long scarf to wrap around their face. I remember Buck always had a red scarf that he used. One night Jody Ridley's late brother, Biddle, and I were watching Simmons power sliding through turns one and two on his way to a dominant half-track win. The tail of Buck's long red scarf was blowing out the driver's window about two feet and I remember telling Biddle that he reminded me of the "Red Baron".

The first few races in 1970 saw Simmons continue his reign as "King of Dixie". Even though he was traveling a lot, when he raced at Dixie Speedway he was still the man to beat. That year saw six different drivers take the checkered flag. Buck again dominated with nine wins, another future NDLMHOF driver Doug Kenimer (2005) had six victories, Leon Sells had three wins, Charlie Mincey had two, and Charlie Padgett also had a win. It took Jody Ridley about a third of that season, but he ended up beating Simmons for the first of his three checkered flags that year.

BY GARY L. PARKER

Ridley later said, "Beating Buck that first time at Dixie was one of my all-time favorite wins."

Simmons went on to be a force in Dirt Late Model racing for many years. He won races all over the country, and was a dominant force in the first national touring series for Dirt Late Models - Robert Smawley's NDRA. He won the 1981 NDRA Championship and was the series' all-time wins leader with 23 victories. He ended his career with 1,012 feature wins, last racing in 2003 in the Gerald Voyles John Deere green #41.

Stan Massey eventually eclipsed Simmons' 46 career wins at Dixie with 69 checkered flags of his own at the now venerable Georgia facility. But the fact is that Simmons dominated the first two years of racing at Dixie Speedway like no driver has since that time. Even today, 47 years later, Dixie Speedway race fans still talk fondly about Buck. Buck Simmons will always be known to many a race fan, and driver alike, as "The King of Dixie Speedway". Sadly, the racing world lost one of the best Dirt Late Model drivers to ever strap into a race car when Charles Leroy "Buck" Simmons passed away on August 12, 2012.

Chapter Three
THE RISE OF THE NDRA

Before we go into Buck Simmons' days as a successful driver on Robert Smawley's NDRA trail in the next chapter. I think we need to take a quick look at the sad condition dirt late model racing was facing shortly before the National Dirt Racing Association burst onto the scene.

It was the mid-70's and the sport was in trouble, not only in the South, but all over the country. The cost of racing had skyrocketed. The racing purses being offered had failed to keep pace with the rising expenses incurred by both the drivers and car owners. Race teams were lucky if they found a track willing to pay $600 to win a race. Adding fuel to the situation were a number of dishonest track owners and promoters (this was only a small percentage, most were good honest promoters and track owners). During this time many of these "shady" owners and race promoters would announce a certain purse, then would pay only part of it; or in some cases, would skip out with all the money. Thus, rising racing costs, along with a lot of bad promoting of the sport was starting to spell doom for dirt late model racing.

In the mid-70's a Kingsport, Tennessee businessman and promoter by the name of Robert Smawley entered the dirt late model racing scene. Over the years, Smawley had promoted several motorcycle races throughout the Southeast. In addition, he had briefly raced dirt cars, before an accident ended that short lived career. However, in his short racing career, Robert was able to see just how bad the dirt racing situation was throughout the entire country.

In 1976 all that was about to change. That year a Georgia dirt late model star by the name of Doug Kenimer became Smawley's "NDRA Ambassador" and went on a racing "vacation" throughout a large part of the country. Doug was able to gain valuable inside information from the drivers and race teams in several parts of the country. Kenimer brought this information back and it was very instrumental to Smawley in organizing and making his NDRA series a reality. At the time many a driver and car owner looked to Smawley as the man who could lead them to the "Promised Land" of dirt late model racing.

Georgia racing great, Doug Kenimer. Doug played a big part in helping Robert Smawley lay the groundwork for his NDRA series. (Photo from the Robert Smawley collection.)

Drivers from all over the country were taking notice of Smawley's proposed "Travelin' Dirt Show." Asphalt drivers from the North, like Larry Moore and Rodney Combs, were planning to travel South and compete on dirt for the large purses Robert was promising to pay. Even the asphalt chassis guru, Beaverton, Michigan's, Ed Howe was bringing converted asphalt race cars to compete on the South's clay ovals.

A number of drivers felt that if Robert held true to his promises, this new dirt late model series just might save the sport. Many drivers were skeptical at first; but at the same time wanted the NDRA to succeed. For example, Georgia racing star C.L. Pritchett, winner of the 1978 NDRA Reed's Cam 100 at Cherokee (SC) Speedway said, "After racing around on these little-bitty tracks for years, it's nice to get some publicity and make some decent money for winning a race." After his Cherokee win he was asked how it felt to win an NDRA event. A smiling Pritchett said, "It feels $10,000 good."

Ever the showman, Robert Smawley gives C.L. Pritchett a victory kiss after Pritchett won a NDRA race at Cherokee (SC) Speedway. Pritchett was asked how it felt to win an NDRA race. He said, "It feels $10,000 good." (Photo from the Robert Smawley collection.)

Another Georgia driver I have known for many years, Charles Hughes said of new series, "Dirt racing is coming back because of Smawley's series. I know him personally and I feel he will do what he says he will do." Hughes went on to say, "So far he has done what he told the drivers and track owners he would do." In closing Charles said, "Drivers can now make money running a race car, whereas before it was hard to do, if you could at all."

Georgia dirt star, Charles Hughes, in his #39 Camaro. (Photo provided by Charles Hughes.)

Even Buck Simmons saw the NDRA as the new bright spot for dirt late model racing. Buck said of the new series, "I plan on running all of Robert's events for his first season. If he does as promised, the drivers need to support him because he will be good for the future of dirt racing."

Finally, Old "hard luck" Jerry Inmon of Bruce Mississippi said, "In 1978, I won more races than anybody in the country. Since then, thanks to the NDRA, I win less, but win more money." Jerry and his car owner, Dick Stevens, pretty much summed up the feelings of the drivers, car owners, and promoters about to jump on board with the NDRA when they said, "We will run Robert's new series as long as he does what he promises and pays the big purses he says he will pay."

All that was left before the "Rock-em, Sock-em, Travelin' Sideways Dirt Show" became a reality were the two races at the Newport Raceway, held in June and July of 1978. Robert Smawley called those races, his "test races." The first race was known as the "Southeastern Dirt Classic" paying an unheard of $22,000 total purse. That race was won by Buck Simmons, taking home the $10,000 winners check. The final "test race," offering an even bigger purse of $30,000, was won by the man who provided Smawley with much needed facts on the condition of the sport, Doug Kenimer. Doug also won $10,000 for his win, an almost unheard of payout for a dirt racing win at the time. After the two races Robert knew he had a winning series because of the overwhelming driver and race fan response.

A view of the packed grandstands and pit area for Smawley's first "test" race held at the Newport (TN) Speedway in June of 1978. (Photo from the Robert Smawley collection.)

Gary Parker

Now it was on to Jimmy Thomas' East Alabama Motor Speedway and the first "official" NDRA race that was held on August 5, 1978. That race was won by Jimmy Thomas' son, Bobby.

Southeastern Classic Dirt Championship Slated For Newport Raceway, June 9-10

By DENNY DARNELL
Assistant Sports Editor

Kingsport's Robert Smawley has put the world of dirt track racing in a frenzy, especially the drivers from throughout a 14 state area.

Smawley is putting together a racing package for Newport Raceway which will have a total purse in excess of $22,000 with a check of $10,000 going to the winner of a 100-lap feature event.

The racing bonanza, tabbed the Southeastern Classic Dirt Championship, will be held June 9-10 at the Newport facility which is just under a half-mile dirt track.

Action slated Friday includes qualifying plus 25-lap heat races, the number of which will be determined by the total number of entries. On Saturday, there'll be a 50-lap consolation race followed by the 100-lap feature.

The top four qualifiers in Friday's time trials will automatically make the field plus the winner of each heat race. The 24-car field will be completed with the top four finishers in Saturday's consolation race making the field.

"We're expecting anywhere from 150 to 200 cars to be on hand," Smawley said. "That means we'll have about 15 heat races on Friday night and then the 150 laps of racing on Saturday. In all, fans should see about 525 laps of racing during the two-day program.

"Most dirt track drivers are lucky to win $10,000 in a season, much less one race. This event could very well shed a whole new light on dirt track racing.

"To my knowledge, this is the largest dirt track race purse ever in the United States. A race in Ohio last year paid $10,000 to the winner, but the total purse was nowhere near the money posted for this event.

"We'll be paying $2,000 for second which is more than a driver can make at any other track with a win and that would have to be some type of special event."

Kingsporter Robert Smawley is promoter of racing program slated for Newport Raceway, June 9-10, which has a total purse in excess of $22,000.

Presently the track seats 4,233 and Smawley is bringing in additional seating to accommodate 800-1,000 more spectators.

In addition to one of the most competitive fields ever assembled for a dirt track race in the state, Smawley feels fans have something else going for them...the price. The admission for Friday is $5 with Saturday's tickets going for $11. Dual tickets (for both events) can be purchased for $15.

"I think the ticket prices are extremely reasonable for the amount of racing that we have scheduled," Smawley said. "We're expecting to have about 375 laps of racing Friday night following the afternoon's qualifying session and then the 150-lap program on Saturday night.

"And all seats will be reserved. That way, if fans purchase their tickets in advance, they'll know they're assured of a seat."

Sponsoring the event is Valvoline Oil of Ashland, Ky.

The Classic is limited to V-8 late model open competition cars. Major rules governing the event are: no straight axles; fuel must be gas only; cars must have a transmission; no top-mounted spoilers; 14-inch tires; and standard safety equipment with fire extinguisher.

"Several drivers are building new engines while some are putting together new cars especially for this event," Smawley said. "Bill Morton has a new $6,000 engine waiting to use in the race while Knoxville's Bill Corum is building a completely new machine.

"This is probably the only race in the history of this area where all 24 starters are capable of winning a race. And it should be a heck of a race with all 100 laps run under green—caution laps will not count. We're expecting as much as half the field to have approximately the same qualifying time."

Drawing for the order of qualifying will be Friday just prior to the 2 p.m. session. Should qualifying times be duplicated, the car attempting the run first will be given the best position.

Smawley has been in contact with drivers from Florida to New York who say they'll be making the trek to Newport to battle for the winner's check.

"A lot of the northern cars will have the new automatic transmissions," Smawley said. "It'll be interesting to see just how well they work here. We also expect some of the drivers from the asphalt circuit to enter as minimal changes would be necessary to run on dirt."

In addition to the $22,000 purse, there's more money available in contingency money. Smawley has set June 11th as the rain date.

The ticket outlet in Kingsport for the Southeastern Classic Dirt Championship is Stock Car Parts Warehouse on Eastman Road.

Chapter Four
BUCK'S NDRA YEARS THRU 1981

The late Summer of 1978 saw the beginning of the first national touring series for dirt late models. For months Robert Smawley had been the focus of the dirt racing world with his newly formed National Dirt Racing Association (the NDRA). Robert had recruited several big name track owners and promoters from throughout the country to join with him in his new ground breaking series. Also on board were many of the nation's top late model drivers from both dirt and asphalt; as well as thousands of excited race fans.

The stage was now set for Smawley to transform the sport into what many have called the "Golden Age of Dirt Late Model Racing." Robert's "Travelin' Dirt Show" would go on to make national stars out of regional drivers. It also changed forever the regional view most race fans had of the sport. Finally, Smawley found new ways to promote dirt racing. He obtained national sponsorships from companies like, Winter's Performance Products, Hoosier Tires, and Lunati Cams to provide programs that included, a driver points fund, as well as national advertising for his races. So, the entire dirt racing nation was watching as Smawley and his staff rolled into the East Alabama Motor Speedway on August 5, 1978 for their first "official" race.

Buck Simmons had been racing on both dirt and asphalt as the 1978 racing season came to an end. According to Simmons, his main focus in 1979 would be on dirt in Robert

A smiling Robert Smawley in the Winters pace car. (Photo provided by David Chobat.)

Smawley's NDRA series. Buck said, "My decision to race entirely on dirt in 1979 was due solely on the amount of money that could be made following Smawley's new series."

Even before the start of Smawley's first official NDRA event, Simmons had already won the first of what Robert called his "test races. " It was called, the Southeastern Dirt Classic Championship held at the Newport (TN) Speedway. It offered an unheard of total purse of $22,000, with the winner of the 100 lap event receiving a $10,000 check from Smawley.

Because of the late start to the series only five races were ran in 1978. The '79 part of the schedule would include those five races along with eight other scheduled events, ending with a June 30th race at the Anderson (SC) Motor Speedway.

As the '79 season was about to start Buck had missed only one of the NDRA races held so far. At the time Simmons was driving one of the new revolutionary Jig-A-Lo chassis race cars out of Phenix City, Alabama; built by the innovative race car builder and track promoter, Jimmy Thomas. Thomas had teamed Simmons with his two sons, Billy and Bobby. The elder Thomas felt Buck would be the veteran influence his sons needed to further their racing careers with his new racing chassis company.

Here is Buck talking with his car owner Jimmy Thomas (in Jimmy's Speed Shop t-shirt) before an NDRA race. (Photo provided by Wayne Wells.)

Simmons would score the first of his NDRA wins in the $30,000 "Valvoline 100" on March 31, 1979 at East Alabama Motor Speedway; the place where the series got its official start the year before. Simmons was the fast qualifier for the race, turning the 3/8 mile dirt track at 17.29.

The first real action of the race occurred on lap thirteen, Buck was able to drive under the Thomas brothers who got trapped in lap traffic that included Doug Kenimer and Ronnie Johnson. From there it was clear sailing for Simmons for the remaining 87 laps. It was a 1-2-3 finish for Jimmy Thomas' revolutionary new Jig-A-Lo chassis race cars, as Bobby and Billy Thomas finished second and third. Rounding out the top five were, Kenny Brightbill and Leon Archer. After receiving a check for the $10,000 winner's share in victory lane Simmons had praise for the flagman. He said, "The flagman did a great job moving the lapped cars over so I could get through the traffic."

Simmons enjoys the moment in victory lane after winning the 1979 NDRA "Valvoline 100" at East Alabama Motor Speedway. That's Jimmy Thomas, Buck, and Robert Smawley, along with two NDRA Trophy Queens. (Photo provided by Wayne Wells.)

That win was followed by another win on April 14th in the "Winter's 100" at Lavonia (GA) Speedway (Charlie's Raceway), a track where Buck has enjoyed a lot of success over the years.

In that race Simmons was again the fast qualifier with a lap of 18.86 on Lavonia's high red clay banks. When the green flag came out Buck took the point on the start, and after a few laps it became apparent to the big crowd that there was no stopping Simmons on this night. He led the entire 100 laps, lapping all but the next three finishers. Only Loveland, Ohio's Rodney Combs, who finished second, kept it from being another 1-2-3 finish for Jig-A-Lo chassis. It was Billy Thomas, Bobby Thomas, and local Georgia dirt star, Bud Lunsford rounding out the top five. After the win Simmons joined Leon Archer as the only two time winners on Smawley's high dollar dirt circuit.

The 1980 Winter's Pro National Series made its first stop of the season at the Wythe Raceway in Wytheville, Virginia on July 14, 1979. The '80 season was going to be a long one for the NDRA. Robert had scheduled races from July 14, 1979 until the October 26, 1980 finale at the Volunteer Speedway in Bull's Gap, Tennessee. He did this in order to get his series in line with most race track's normal racing season, April through October.

Smawley chose the big half-mile dirt oval at Wytheville for the "Roscoe's Racing 100." It proved to be a good choice, as over 6,000 excited race fans packed this raceway nestled in the hills of this small Southwest Virginia community. Two Ohio drivers, Larry Moore and Rodney Combs, brought the 24 car starting field to the green flag. It was Combs who took the lead on the first lap; holding it until lap seven when Moore got by him and steadily pulled out to a big lead. However, nine caution flags kept the field bunched up all day. An unusually high number of cars would fall out of the race that day. One driver who had a fast car all day was the 1979 NDRA Points Champion, Leon Archer. But his chance for a win slipped away with a flat tire. Archer pitted and returned to the race, finishing in eight position.

Moore was in control until the last of the cautions came out with a few laps to go. Buck Simmons, who had ran a steady race all day suddenly found himself in the runner-up spot with only two laps to go. Moore couldn't shake Simmons as the two headed for the white flag. Going into a turn Moore made a mistake and Simmons was there to take advantage. Simmons came under him and went on to take the checkered flag and the trip to victory lane. Moore was clearly the fastest car all day; but as the old saying goes, "You gotta lead the last lap." Rounding out the top five were, Rodney Combs, Freddy Smith, and Jerry Inmon. This was Buck's third win of the NDRA series, putting him again in a tie with Leon Archer for the most wins with three each.

Buck takes another NDRA win and enjoys a moment with Robert Smawley in victory lane. (Photo provided by Wayne Wells.)

Simmons had raced on asphalt successfully for a number years all over the South. He ran asphalt's Famous Snowball Derby on several occasions, finishing second in 1977 to fellow Georgia driver, Ronnie Sanders. Even with that Buck had been saying for years, "I have always wondered what it would feel like to go a 190 mph."

In 1979, Kennie Childers and his NASCAR Kencoal Mining race team gave Buck that chance. During his short NASCAR career, from 11/04/1979 to 5/04/1980, Simmons ran a total of eight NASCAR Cup events. He raced at, Bristol, Darlington, Martinsville, Rockingham, Talladega, Ontario, and Atlanta. Buck seemed to be doomed to bad luck, scoring five DNF's in his eight races. However, he won the pole at Ontario Speedway in a K&N Pro West Series race. His best NASCAR Cup finish was a 14th place finish at Atlanta Motor Speedway.

This is the Kencoal Mining/Kennie Childers #12 that Simmons drove during his brief NASCAR stint in 1979 and early 1980. (Photo is a Robert Turner photo.)

After his brief stint in NASCAR Buck said, "I was a driver that didn't know a lot about race car set-ups (more about this later from Larry Moore and Barry Wright). In NASCAR you have to have driver feed back to the race team, I just didn't know what to tell them." Simmons continued, "Another reason for me coming back to dirt was, I couldn't go off and stay all week, I just didn't have the money." He said in closing,

"That NASCAR racing was about to leave me eating out of the garbage can." With that now behind him, Simmons returned to his first love, dirt late model racing.

Since returning to dirt racing and the NDRA series, it had been twelve months since Simmons had won a series event. All that was about to change on July 26, 1980 at Bull's Gap, Tennessee's Volunteer Speedway. To the delight of a lot of race fans Simmons had returned to the NDRA, now driving the Carrie Coal Company race car of Virginia's Darrell Monk.

Volunteer proved to be a very fast track for the "Looney Chevrolet 100." A total of five cars broke the track record of "Little" Bill Corum. In the end it was Freddy Smith in the #00 with a fast time of 14.82 on the pole, with Simmons in the Monk ride starting on the outside front row. As the green waved Buck charged to the lead followed closely by Smith. As the race settled in it became apparent to the overflow crowd that Simmons was the class of the 24 car starting field. He went on to lead the entire 100 laps as only the B&D Industrial Boilers Camaro of Smith was able to challenge him for the lead on a couple of occasions. Rounding out the top five behind Simmons and Smith were, Chattanooga's Ronnie Johnson finishing third in a thrilling battle with the fourth place finisher, Larry Moore. Leon Archer in his famous #222 Camaro was fifth.

It was a happy Simmons, Darrell Monk, and crew in victory lane. Buck said, "This race team needed this one, and I needed it also to get back on track in this series."

Buck scored another win in the very next NDRA event at the Jackson (TN) Fairgrounds Speedway on August 8th. Since returning to the series Simmons had served notice that he was again going to be one of the drivers to beat.

Later, as the '80 racing season entered its final months, Simmons made a switch to another race team. This time he

Buck celebrates with Smawley and Trophy Queeen, Eva Taylor, after a win in the Darrel Monk #41. (Photo provided by Michael Edwards.)

would team with Ohio late model star Rodney Combs under the Tri-City Aluminum banner. The team was owned by Jim Erp of Ocala, Florida. They had identical Camaros; Buck drove the white #41, while Combs drove his familiar white #5. It appeared to the dirt racing world that Erp had just assembled probably the best race team to hit the NDRA since it began a little over two years earlier.

Jim Erp brought his new race team to Mickey Swims' famed Dixie Speedway for the track's inaugural National Dirt Championship. Mickey had decided to pay a large purse for this race, with $16,000 going to the winning driver. Swims' plan was to add a $1,000 increase to the winner's share each year of his track's final event. (The event later became known as the Hav-A-Tampa Shootout).

On October 5, 1980 the stage was set for Smawley's "travelin" dirt show" to roar into Mickey's Dixie Speedway for a big day of racing. Robert had brought the best of his regular dirt warriors including, Larry Moore, Charlie Swartz, Rodney Combs, Tom Helfrich, Buck Simmons and others; to do battle with some of the region's best, such as Leon Sells, Bud Lunsford, Stan Massey, Fulmer Lance, and several others from the Southeast.

Billy Teegarden was the fast qualifier for the 100 lap "Flexi-Flyer National Championship," setting a new track record in the process.

As the green flag waved on the star studded field Combs was able to take command, in his Tri-City Aluminum #5. His teammate, Buck Simmons, was content to run fifth in the early going in his #41 machine. A short time later, Simmons made his move and passed several cars and found himself running in second position behind Combs.

Combs and Simmons ran nose-to-tail for several laps. However, a caution slowed the field on lap 43, giving Larry Moore a chance to make a tire change. When the race returned to green, the big crowd watched as Moore moved ever closer to the two front runners. Combs appeared to be in command, leading the first 96 laps. As the laps were winding down, a dogfight between the two Erp Teammates began to take place. Both caught Tennessee driver Gary Hall on lap 97, Hall moved to the low groove to let the leaders pass. Combs went high to pass Hall. It was then that Buck made one of his trademark moves. He threaded the needle between Combs and Hall and charged to the lead. Combs tried to regain the lead, but could not get by as Buck took the checkered flag and the winners check for $16,200.

The standing room only crowd had witnessed a thrilling finish, with one of the all time crowd favorites at Dixie coming home a winner. The top ten that day were, Simmons, Combs, Larry Moore, L.D. Ottinger, Charlie Swartz, Tom Helfrich, H.E. Vineyard, Rusty Wilson, Jerry Inmon, and Leon Sells.

WINTER'S PERFORMANCE PRO-NATIONAL SERIES PRESENTS THE

FAD'S

100

U.S.A'S RICHEST DIRT TRACK RACE

OCTOBER 3-4-5

$16,000 TO WIN

DIXIE SPEEDWAY
Atlanta, Georgia
(Woodstock)
Route 3, Hwy. 92

The 1981 NDRA season, now known as the NDRA/Schlitz Pro National Series, started out as a bit of a surprise for Simmons. Teammate Rodney Combs had decided to again concentrate on Winter racing in Australia. When I was writing the book on the history of the NDRA, *The ROCK-EM, SOCK-EM TRAVELIN' SIDEWAYS DIRT SHOW*, Rodney told me, "I raced in Australia from 1978 until 1993." Combs continued, "I won something like a 1000 races there. I was perhaps the most recognized American driver there, even more than Richard Petty."

However, Combs did race some in the states that year, winning a Southeastern Winter Nationals event at Volusia (FLA) Speedway and a 100 lap event at the Newport

(TN) Speedway. But in '81 it was clear he was focusing on racing in Australia.

In '81 Jim Erp had teamed with Midwest racing star, Larry Moore. Over the years, Moore had driven race cars for some of the best including, Ed Howe, Bobby Paul, C..J. Rayburn, and even some of his own race cars.

Upon teaming with Erp and his Tri-City Aluminum team, Moore insisted on hiring Simmons to drive a second car for the team. Moore said, "I brought my crew chief, Steve Smith along, putting him with Simmons." Larry then said, "I met Simmons at my first NDRA race at Atomic (TN) Speedway in 1978, a race I won." Moore continued, "As Buck and I raced more and more, it amazed me how little he knew about chassis setups." Larry went on, "At the time we formed the Erp/Moore team I was a developmental driver for Hoosier Racing Tires, so needless to say, Buck and I did a lot of testing." In closing Larry said, "No matter what we did to Buck's car he drove the same lap speeds. He is one of the few driver's that had the natural ability to adapt his driving style to whatever the race car was doing."

A couple of years ago the ever funny Harley "Fuzzy" Orange, the former NDRA flagman and pit steward, probably gave me the best ever description of the way Simmons set up a race car. Fuzzy said, "Old Buck would climb in, sit down, wiggle his ass in the seat til he felt comfortable, strap himself in, and then he would lean forward and tell the race car, you are going to be my [Buck's] best friend tonight."

The 1981 NDRA/Schlitz Pro National tour proved to a "season for the ages" turned in by the Tri-City Aluminum race team. The team won an amazing 17 of the 28 events. It was a year that left the competition wishing that both Simmons and Moore had followed Rodney Combs to Australia. The season was dominated by Simmons and Moore like no other before or after.

Simmons, in the Tri-City Aluminum #41, does battle with Leon Archer. (Photo provided by Gene Lefler.)

In addition to winning the NDRA Points Championship, Buck scored a season high 11 wins on the NDRA trail; while his teammate, Moore, added another six checkered flags that season (according to Dirt on Dirt). What stands out most about Buck's incredible '81 season was the almost total dominance he displayed from, his win on June 13th at Paducah (KY) International Raceway to his win at the same track on August 22. Buck won an amazing 9 of those 14 races. The win streak included four checkered flags in a row during an eight day span from August 14th to August 22nd. Those wins occurred at, Log Cabin Raceway at Rocky Mount, VA., on the 14th; Wythe Raceway at Wytheville, Va., on the 16th; Santa Fe Speedway, Willow Springs, Ill., on the 20th; and Paducah (KY) International Raceway, on the 22nd.

Let's now take a closer look at three of Simmons' wins from his historic '81 championship season.

It was Friday night, June 19, 1981 at the Florence Speedway in Union, Kentucky. Robert Smawley, with all his showbiz pizzas, had introduced his newest national sponsor, the Schlitz Brewing Company, to the Northern Kentucky crowd gathered for his 75 lap NDRA/Schlitz Pro National points race. As with most of his events, Robert had a standing room only crowd of excited race fans waiting for start of the big race. The trophy queens, including Miss NDRA Eva Taylor, were there; an elite field of the nation's best dirt stars, representing eight states, were there. Included in the field was probably the hottest race team in the series, Larry Moore and Buck Simmons in the Tri-City Aluminum Red Camaros.

With qualifying completed, Larry Moore was the fastest qualifier with a lap of 18.64. Buck Simmons also found himself at the front of the field after winning his heat race. So, all that was left was the waving of the green flag to start the race.

As the 22 car starting field took the green flag, the cars raced cleanly through turns one and two and down the back stretch; as most of the field went cleanly through turns three and four, the #B3 of Randy Boggs suddenly went hard into the turn three guard rail and the red flag quickly came out.

Since the first lap was not completed under green, the field was restarted. Four drivers were unable to continue, they were, Randy Boggs, Jack Boggs, Bruce Gould, and Don Seaborn. After the cars were relined the flagman waved the green. Once again Moore jumped to the lead, followed closely by Simmons, Freddy Smith, Pat Patrick, Billy Teegarden, and Rodney Combs. However, on lap 30 Moore blew a tire after scraping the guard rail and stopped on the track, causing the second caution of the race.

Moore quickly changed the tire and rejoined the tail end of the field.

On the restart Simmons found himself in the lead followed closely by Pat Patrick, Combs, Teegarden, and Mike Duvall. It stayed that way until lap 45, when Moore caused his second caution of the night. This time he had a broken tie rod after making his way back to eighth place, and was finished for the night.

On the final restart of the night, Simmons was leading followed by a now determined Pat Patrick. Simmons was now challenged on almost every lap, Patrick trying him high one lap and then low the next. During the final laps of the race the excited crowd came to their feet as Simmons and Patrick ran side-by-side all the way around the big half-mile oval while going thru lapped traffic.

As the two dirt warriors came to the finish, it was Simmons taking the checkered flag as Patrick finished second, inches from Buck's rear bumper. The remainder of the top five included, Teegarden, Combs, and Jerry Inmon.

Simmons was all smiles as he received the winner's check for $3,000 and the big race trophy from Miss NDRA, Eva Taylor. At this point he was now clearly the favorite for the season's points championship.

The Tri-City Aluminum race team had momentum on their side as they rolled into the ultra fast Atomic Speedway just outside of Knoxville, Tennessee for a big NDRA holiday weekend of racing on July 3rd. Larry Moore had scored two wins so far in the '81 season; while his teammate, Simmons, had won three of the last four series points races. This included the last series race at the Tazewell (TN) Speedway on June 25th. In that race it was the "Buck and Larry show," as Simmons beat teammate Larry Moore for the win.

With the qualifying completed at Atomic it was Kentucky's Jack Boggs who found himself on the pole, with Simmons in his #41 red Camaro along side on the front row.

The Tri-City Aluminum race team, Buck Simmons in #41, and Larry Moore, #14. (Photo provided by Bill Hall.)

The sell out crowd rose to its feet as the flagman waved the green to start the 100 lap event. Boggs in the #B4 jumped to the lead, but as the cars were going thru turns one and two, local dirt star H.E. Vineyard tangled with another car in turn two and caution came out before the field completed a lap. It proved to be a lucky break for Simmons as he was able to pit and have a skipping carburetor checked. With the track set to go back to green Simmons again joined Boggs on the front row; and as the cars came out of turn four and by the big Pepsi scoring tower the green again came out. This time Simmons was able to put his famous power slide on Boggs and take the lead going down the back straight-a-way.

Simmons was clearly the fastest car in the field on this night. However, fifteen caution flags kept the cars tightly bunched throughout the race. This kept Buck from "leaving town" on the rest of the field. In the end it was Simmons making his fourth trip in five races to victory lane. A happy Simmons collected the $3,000 winner's share from NDRA Series President, Robert Smawley. The remainder of the top five were, Jack Boggs, Freddy Smith, Jack Trammell, and Jerry Inmon.

In late July of '81 Simmons started piloting a new light weight race car for Cowpens, South Carolina chassis builder, Barry Wright. The car weighted only 2,000 pounds, race ready. Buck had a successful three race stint in the car. In non-series races Simmons scored a win, a second, and a third in the Barry Wright race car. The NDRA weight rule of 2600 pounds kept the Wright car from racing in the series.

So, Buck was now back in the Tri-City Aluminum #41 Camaro for the August 14th Mr. Pibb/NDRA 100 at Log Cabin Raceway and Park at Rocky Mount, Va. It had been almost a month since Simmons' last NDRA win. That series victory came on July 15th at the half-mile Seacrest Speedway in Georgetown, Delaware in the "Kenview Kompetition 100." In that race Simmons took the checkers ahead of Ronnie Miles and Pete Parker.

On this mid-August night at Log Cabin, Simmons was starting in the seventh spot as the flagman waved the green. Larry Moore led the early laps, as Simmons picked off the cars ahead of him one by one. On lap 17 he was able to get by Moore and complete a lap before Mike Duvall, in the Flintstone Flyer, blew an engine. On the restart Simmons took command of the race, as Moore and Leon Archer put on a torrid battle for second. On lap 78 Archer blew the engine in his Barry Wright/Carolina Tools Camaro

As the race went back to green, Simmons was able to find the grip off the corners and took control of the race in the final laps to win the $3,000 series points race. The big crowd was on its feet as Moore and Jack Boggs put on a show for second. In the end it was Moore finishing in the runner-up spot as Boggs took third only inched from Larry's rear bumper.

After Simmons' victory at Log Cabin he would go on to take his final NDRA checkered flags in the next three events. Those three races (mentioned earlier in the chapter) were again, Wythe, Santa Fe, and Paducah.

Simmons won the 1981 NDRA Points Championship in dominant fashion. The final points standings for the season were: Buck Simmons-12,640; Freddy Smith-11,482; Jerry Inmon-10,910; Larry Moore-10,868; and Jack Boggs-9,544.

After winning the '81 NDRA/Schlitz Pro National Series Championship; Simmons would begin a long driver association with Cowpens, South Carolina's Barry Wright Race Cars as the '82 racing season began. As mentioned earlier, he had driven one of Barry Wright's lightweight "outlaw" dirt late models in several non-series races during part of the '81 season.

Since the start of Smawley's NDRA series, Simmons had been a consistent top five finisher in the points races. In '79 he finished second to Leon Archer; fourth in '80 behind eventual winner Larry Moore; and he won the title in '81. It was now the beginning of the '82 season and the racing veteran was starting his fourth NDRA season. It appeared Buck was now focused and ready to try and win a second series title in 1982.

Wayne Wells, the NDRA Tech Inspector, has a word with Buck Simmons during a race. (Photo provided by Wayne Wells.)

After another NDRA win, Buck shares a victory drink. (Photo from the Robert Smawley collection.)

Chapter Five
BUCK'S NDRA YEARS 1982 TO 1985

The 1982 season proved that Buck Simmons was one of the most consistent drivers on the NDRA Series tour, since its beginning in the late Summer of '78.

Buck Simmons (back to camera) and Larry Moore (blue jacket) talk things over as track officials work on the Silverdome track. (Photo from the Robert Smawley collection.)

It was early March of '82 and Simmons, along with most of Smawley's NDRA touring regulars, found themselves at the Pontiac Silverdome for the big $50,000 Budweiser "Super Bowl Of Dirt." For months, the event had been receiving a lot of national coverage. It would be the first time that dirt late models had raced indoors. With qualifying over, Buck

A flyer from the "Super Bowl of Dirt" at the Pontiac Silverdome held on March 8, 1982. (Flyer provided by Bob Markos.)

had set the fast time with a lap of 13.50 on the tiny 1/5 mile dirt oval. However, Simmons ended the night finishing seventh in a race won by Kentucky's Jack Boggs. Boggs took the $8,000 winner's check before an excited crowd of 30,000 fans in the Silverdome.

On May 8th the much publicized "World's Fair 75" was held in conjunction with the 1982 World's Fair in Knoxville, Tennessee. Ohio's Rodney Combs would come home a winner in the $7,000 to win NDRA event at Smoky Mountain Speedway in nearby Maryville, Tennessee. He was followed across the finish line by two Georgia drivers, Leon Archer and Buck Simmons.

Haubstadt, Indiana, dirt star Tom Helfrich. Helfrich would go on to score the win in another big NDRA event at Smoky Mountain (TN) Speedway. Helfrich won the first NDRA Invitational there in 1984. (Photo from the Robert Smawley Collection.)

The World's Fair race started a string of top five finishes that would find Simmons out of the top five on only four occasions. Also, during the '82 season he had only two finishes out of the top ten. Those were, a 14th place finish at the Wythe (VA) Raceway; and a 21st place finish in the season's first race at Metrolina (NC) Speedway. Simmons scored an amazing sixteen top five finishes, including two series wins in '82.

The two NDRA/Schlitz Pro National Series wins were scored in the "Buckeye" state; and on back-to back nights in early August.

On Friday August 6th Simmons showed up at Portsmouth, Ohio's Southern Ohio Raceway with his new Barry Wright/Carolina Tools #41 Firebird. Right out of the hauler, Simmons gave notice to the big crowd and his fellow drivers that he would be the one to beat on this night. On his second lap of qualifying he set a new track record, turning the half-mile dirt facility at 17.53.

Later, as the 24 car starting field came out of turn four to take the green flag, Buck jumped to the lead on the first lap of the Shaker Coal 100. He put his #41 in a power slide thru turns one and two and pulled out to a big lead down the back straight-a-way over Jack Boggs, Rodney Combs, and Delmas Conley. Simmons was putting on a driving clinic through the first 25 laps. The only move made behind Buck's Firebird was, Combs taking second from Boggs.

At the lap 51 fuel stop it was Simmons, Combs, Pat Patrick, John Mason, and Boggs. The race returned to green and it was basically a repeat of the first 50 laps; as Buck steadily pulled away from the field until a caution came out on lap 83 for an accident back in the field.

When the race returned to green, Buck put his Barry Wright Firebird on cruise control for the final 17 laps. It was a flag to flag win for Simmons over, Combs in his J.D. Stacy Firebird; Pat Patrick's Stricker Auto Parts Camaro; Jack Boggs in the Shaker Coal Camaro; and Donnie Seaborn in the A.J. Stephens Excavating race car.

Saturday August 7th found Simmons and his Barry Wright flying Firebird just up the road at Chilicothe, Ohio's Atomic Speedway. An excited crowd was waiting for the start of the NDRA/Schlitz 100. It appeared to all involved that it was going to be a "same song second verse" night; as Simmons again was the fastest car in qualifying, turning a lap of 15.40.

The flagman waved the green and it was off to the races for Buck Simmons. He charged to the lead over Pat Patrick, Rodney Combs, Jack Boggs, and Dave Robinson. A short time later the night's first caution came out on lap 7 for an accident involving Larry Scott. The field returned to green, but four laps later Boggs stopped on the track in turn four, causing the night's second yellow.

On the restart Simmons still held the lead followed by Pat Patrick, and Combs. Lap 36 saw another caution as Jim Taylor spun out in a turn. After the field was restarted it ran green until the Lap 51 fuel stop.

When the green came back out it was Simmons on the point followed closely by Patrick, Delmas Conley, and the Flintstone Flyer of Mike Duvall. Simmons and the next four cars started to pull away from the rest of the field as the race wore on. The night's real excitement started on lap 76; as the Atomic defending track champion, Delmas Conley, started to charge toward the front. Conley moved to second behind Simmons on lap 86 and the big crowd came to its feet as Conley passed Simmons for the lead. However, before a lap was completed the caution came out, putting Conley back in second place. As the green waved again, Conley waged a crowd pleasing battle with Buck for several laps until an over heating engine forced Conley from the race.

As the green came out for the final few laps Simmons was able to stay a few car lengths ahead of Patrick, Combs, Duvall, and Robinson as the checkered flag waved. It was a two-for-two weekend for Simmons and Barry Wright. A happy Simmons and his crew received the NDRA winner's check in victory lane.

The '82 season would mark the last time Buck would finish in the top five in the points for the NDRA series. He finished fourth that year.

In 1983 the Simmons/Barry Wright race team still ran most of the series races. In the races he ran in '83, his best finish was a fourth at one of his all time favorite tracks, the Dixie (GA) Speedway. That race was the NDRA/Dixie Nationals won by local dirt star Stan Massey. In the series races he competed in that year he finished out of the top ten only twice. That was a 26th place finish at the Hagerstown (MD) Speedway, and an 11th at the Dodge Nationals at I-70 in Odessa, MO. Buck finished ninth in NDRA points in 1983.

During the '83 season it was apparent, that the Simmons/Wright race team had shifted their focus to running late models and "outlaw" wedge late models in the Carolina's and Georgia areas. There were quite a few big money non-series races during the time.

Some of Simmons' non-series late model and outlaw wins in '83 were, the Shrine 100 at Cherokee (SC) Speedway; the Northeast GA Championship at Lavonia (GA) Speedway; the Riverside S.C. 75; the Mello Yellow Invitational at Cherokee Speedway; and the Cherokee Speedway 75.

The '84 NDRA season saw Simmons run the majority of Smawley's series events. His best finish was at the Dixie

Nationals at Woodstock, GA., where he finished second to Clarksville, Tennessee's Jeff Purvis. Simmons finished the '84 NDRA season sixth in series points.

Buck Simmons #41 and Jeff Purvis #15 doing battle in wedge race cars at Atomic (TN) Speedway. Note the speed on the scoreboard, WOW. (Photo provided by Gene Lefler.)

In a recent phone conversation with Barry Wright, he said, "Going into the '84 season, Buck and I had decided to focus our attention on the popular "outlaw circuit" in North and South Carolina, and Georgia because of the large purses a lot of tracks in the area were paying." Barry continued, "If the NDRA races fit our schedule we ran them."

The '84 season also saw the Simmons/Wright race team put more focus on the "wedge" outlaw late models. This is evidenced by the non-series wins that year. Some of those wedge car wins included, the Wedge 60; the Outlaw Spectacular; and the Firecracker 200 all at Concord, NC.

According to Barry Wright, "The '85 season saw our team focus mainly on the wedge outlaw race cars." Barry continued, "We again raced mostly in the Carolina's and Georgia."

Simmons, in Barry Wright wedge race car, powers thru a turn on the high side. (Photo provided by Gene Lefler.)

They won a number of big outlaw events in '85. Some of those included, the Labor Day 100 at Concord, NC; the Budweiser 50 at Lancaster, SC; and the Wedge Invitational at the legendary Cherokee Speedway in Gaffney, SC.

During the '85 season I was teaching anthropology at USC-Union and saw Simmons win a number of weekly outlaw races at Cherokee and at the I-85 Speedway in Greer, SC. He even won the Shriner's race that year at the Laurens Speedway in Laurens, SC. I was living in Laurens at the time, only about two miles from the track.

Barry said, "We didn't focus on the NDRA series in '85, but decided to compete in the big invitational race at Kingsport, Tennessee in mid-October. We would be representing I-85 Speedway in that event."

Barry Wright then said, "Because we had been racing the outlaw cars so much, we had to build a smaller race car to meet the NDRA rules." Wright continued, "We took a two year old racing chassis and put a new rear suspension under the race car." Barry went on to say, "During that last weekend

An ad for the 2nd annual Stroh's/NDRA Invitational held at the Kingsport (TN) Speedway, won by Buck simmons. (Ad provided by Bob Markos.)

and the early part of the week leading up to the Kingsport race, we worked our tails off to get that car ready."

As the weekend of the Stroh's/NDRA $250,000 Invitational approached; a total of 142 drivers from 25 states descended upon NDRA President Robert Smawley's hometown of Kingsport, Tennessee for the four day event.

At the time almost no one knew that this would be the last big extravaganza for Smawley's "travelin' dirt show."

The site for the NDRA's ultimate dirt battle would be the tight and narrow one-third mile Kingsport Speedway. The big money event had $20,000 of the purse going to the winning driver. In addition, one of Smawley's newest national sponsors, Dutch Treats, was putting up $10,000 for the driver who turned the fastest lap.

Practice began on Thursday October 10th, with qualifying set for the next day. Buck Simmons was no stranger to the speedway having ran some modified races in the early '60's and late models in the '70's there. He had raced on both the Kingsport's dirt and then the asphalt surfaces. So it came as no surprise when Buck walked away with the Dutch Treats $10,000 Pole Award, after turning a lap of 16.080 – a full tenth of a second faster than second place qualifier, Arkansas' Tommy Joe Pauschert.

With about 200 cars a day racing on the track on both Thursday and Friday, the track turned black with tire rubber and was hard as asphalt. This caught a lot of drivers and race teams off guard with many spending all day Saturday trying to find the right set-up for the six do or die Saturday heat races.

Simmons was in the catbird's seat as he had the pole all rapped up and was set to go in Sunday's 100 lap event. A rain shower early on Sunday morning made the track even more abrasive.

It was Sunday October 13, 1985, the crowd was there, the media was there, and even a few television stations were on hand as the flagman waved the green on the star studded field.

Simmons, in his Barry Wright red #41 took the lead on lap one, and would go on to lead the entire 100 lap event. After a few laps two things became apparent to almost everyone present; it was going to be a dusty race and there would be little, if any, passing.

Buck takes the low groove during the 1985 Stroh's/NDRA Invitational on his way to the checkered flag. (Photo provided by Gene Lefler.)

Only Charles Powell III seemed to have the ability to pass in the early stages. Later, Jeff Purvis and Scott Bloomquist were able to gain some positions late in the race. Otherwise, it was a typical follow the leader one groove dry slick track.

When Simmons took the checkered flag on lap 100; he was followed across the finish line by, Tommy Joe Pauschert, Jeff Purvis, Freddy Smith, and Scott Bloomquist in fifth.

Later, a tired Simmons said of his victory, "I just stayed on my toes all day and tried to run as near the bottom as I could. The track was a racers nightmare, no way you could pick up enough speed to pass on the top."

It was a smiling and happy Simmons and crew who received the $20,000 winner's check and another $10,000 check from Dutch Treats. When asked about his victory, Simmons said, "This $30,000 weekend for me and the car owner, that's the most money I have ever won for a weekend of racing."

As Simmons headed home to Baldwin, Georgia, his very successful NDRA career was over. He had left his mark on Smawley's NDRA, winning the 1981 Series Championship. He would also go on to become the series all-time wins leader with 23 Victories.

Gary Parker

Chapter Six

THE BARRY WRIGHT YEARS

In 1982 Buck Simmons hooked up with Cowpens, South Carolina's master chassis man, Barry Wright. Together they ran many of Smawley's NDRA races over the next three years.

Simmons $3000 Atomic NDRA Winner

by Tom Clutters

ALMA, OH - Aug. 7 - For the second time in as many nights, Buck Simmons of Baldwin, GA guided his Barry Wright-Carolina Tool number 41 Late Model into victory lane as the defending NDRA champion collected the $3,000 top money in te Schlitz 100 at Atomic Speedway on Saturday night. Simmons had previously won the Shaker Coal Company 100 at Southern Ohio Raceway on Friday night, making it three victories in four nights in his new ride.

As he had done the previous night, Simmons had the fast time during qualifying, posting a 15.40 on his second lap. At the drop of the green in the feature, Buck set out around the three-eighths mile clay oval just ahead of Pat Patrick, Rodney Combs, Jack Boggs and Dave Robinson. Larry Scott of Grand Rapids, OH brought out the first yellow after seven laps and four laps later, Boggs coasted to a stop in turn four, then headed for the pits for quick repairs. Patrick and Combs continued to challenge Simmons for the lead, and the field was closed up on the 18th tour when the caution came out for John Mason, who had a flat tire.

The race continued smoothly through 35 laps, but on the 36th circuit, Jim Taylor and Combs bumped, with Taylor spinning out. After the restart, Simmons charged to the fuel break at lap 51, still in the lead followed by Patrick, Combs, Delmas Conley and Mike Duvall. This five car lead pack began the second half by pulling away from the field somewhat. Boggs, meanwhile, trying to make up the ground lost earlier, tangled with Allan Russell on the 57th circuit, dropping him back once again. On about the 76th lap, Conley began to make his move, getting around Combs for third place and setting out in pursuit of the leaders. Patrick, with his attention focused on Simmons, suddenly found himself in third after Conley passed him on the 80th lap.

The fans, taking note of Conley's daredevil charge, began to stand and cheer as the defending Atomic Champion moved after Simmons. The stands went wild as Delmas got into the lead on lap 86, only to have the yellow flag come out due to debris on the track.

This put Simmons back in front with Conley second, Patrick third and Combs fourth. Conley resumed his chase but trouble developed when his number 71 Firebird began to overheat and eventually forced him to the infield. At the finish, it was Simmons, Patrick, Combs and Duvall in the top four positions, followed by Robinson, Boggs, Taylor, Scott, George Glick and Bob Crace, Sr.

George Harbour posted a win in the Sprint heat with Steve Thornton and Bob Dean winning the Six Cylinder heats. The features were postponed one week due to foggy conditions.

This article is about the second of two nights of Buck's back-to-back Ohio wins during the 1982 NDRA season. (Article provided by Bob Markos.)

As mentioned in an earlier chapter, Simmons won back to back NDRA races in Ohio on August 6th and 7th of '82. In a recent interview Barry Wright told me, "We also won a $5,000 to win race on Thursday August 5th at Sugar Creek Speedway in Buffalo, South Carolina. Then on the way home from Ohio we stopped by the Tazewell (TN) Speedway and won a race there on Sunday night August 8th." Barry closed by saying, "That was probably one of the most productive weekends Buck and I had together."

In 1985 Simmons won his most prosperous achievement in dirt late model racing: the lucrative $250,000 Stroh's/NDRA Invitational at the Kingsport (TN) Speedway. On October 13, 1985 Simmons, driving a two year old Barry Wright race car with a new suspension system, started from the pole and led all 100 laps of the star studded event. In addition, he won the Dutch Treats Pole Award worth a cool $10,000, and the race that paid $20,000 to the winner. In all Buck took $30,000 back to his Baldwin, Georgia home, in what he called, "A helluva day."

Recently Barry Wright told me, "That was the only NDRA race we ran that year. We had been running wedge race car all over the South and had to build a small dirt race car to meet the NDRA rules." Barry continued, "We worked our tails off to get the car ready for that race."

Wright said, "The mid-'80's was the heyday of the outlaw wedge race cars and that had been our focus since about 1983. There were a lot of big racing purses being offered in the Carolina's and Georgia at the time."

After joining forces in '82, it didn't take Wright long to figure out that Simmons knew almost nothing about setting up a race car (Larry Moore mentioned this in an earlier chapter). Barry told me, "You had to watch Buck in the car on the first lap, to see what the car was doing. If you waited til

Here is Simmons in 1982 at the legendary Pennsboro Speedway in a Barry Wright/Carolina Tool early version of the wedge car. (Photo provided by Gene Lefler.)

the second lap it was too late, Old Buck had already adapted himself to what the race car was doing."

Barry told me a funny story about Buck, he said, "One morning before a race that night, I was changing the engine in the race car." Wright continued, "We we staying in one of those old motels where the doors open to the outside. As I was working I happened to look up and Buck was peeping out of the curtains. He saw me looking and quickly closed them." Barry continued, "A little later the same thing happened again. I knew Buck never got moving til about noon." In closing Barry said with a laugh, "As I was finishing with the last header pipe, here comes Buck, and he said, 'Anything I can do to help, Barry?' I told him get in and crank the car. I found out Simmons also didn't like to work on race cars either."

Some of Simmons' biggest years with Wright were the '84 and '85 racing seasons. It was the height of the "lexan era"

Buck's #41 at an NDRA race in 1984 at Concord, NC. Note the Stroh's NDRA sign in background. The Stroh's Brewing Co. joined forces with Smawley in '84, becomng the NDRA Series' major sponsor. (Photo provided by Gene Lefler.)

and they were winning a lot of wedge outlaw races all over the South. Perhaps their most famous wedge race car was the light weight (about 1,700 pounds) Carolina Tool Company red #41, with all the lexan set-up on it. Wright said, "We won 18 races in a row with the car, mainly in the South Carolina area. I know we won well over 50 races with that car."

Wright said one of the most memorable wins of the '86 season occurred at the Anderson (SC) Speedway. The Simmons/Wright race team were racing both, wedge cars and late models at the time. The hot driver at the time in dirt late models was Clarksville, Tennessee's Jeff Purvis. Purvis was coming off back to back NDRA Series Championships in '84 and '85. In '86 he had won about twelve races in a row, coming into the July 1st race at Anderson. It was the NASCAR Busch All Star Super Series race.

As the 50 lap event got underway, Simmons charged to the lead and led all 50 laps with Purvis nipping at Buck's rear

Here is Simmons at the Chrokee (SC) Speedway at the height of the lexan era. This Barry Wright/Carolina Tools red #41 won 18 races in a row at one point, and over 50 races in all, according to Barry Wright. This was one bad race car, weighing only about 1700 pounds. (Photo provided by Gene Lefler.)

bumper the entire race. The finishing order for the race was, Simmons, Purvis, Ronnie Johnson, Freddy Smith, and C.L. Pritchett completing the top five.

1987 the Simmons/Wright race team continued to race in the Carolina and Georgia areas mainly in dirt late models. One track that they focused on was the historic Cherokee Speedway in Gaffney, South Carolina. A few years earlier, the track had introduced the twin dirt late model feature races. It was a crowd favorite, because the winner of the first feature had to start in the rear of the second, making for some exciting racing. Barry Wright said, "Buck won a number of these races, and on a number of occasions won both." Also, Cherokee Speedway ran two races a month that paid $10,000 to win. Simmons also won a number of those, according to Wright.

In addition to the outlaw races, in both wedge and late model race cars, Simmons also ran a number of Hav-A-Tampa, and STARS Series races during the late 1980's and into the

Simmons Returns to Anderson for All Star Win

By SALUDA SAM
Piedmont, SC

ANDERSON, SC (July 1) — The winner's face was very familiar to Anderson Speedway fans, but, it just hadn't been around lately.

Buck Simmons, one of the top winners at the Anderson track in years past, made a return in fine style, winning the NASCAR Busch All Star Super Series Late Model feature Tuesday night.

Simmons showed he had not forgotten the way around the track as he qualified the fastest and then proceeded to lead all 50 laps of the event to claim $2,300 in prize money.

Jeff Purvis of Clarksville, TN, stayed fairly close in second place and finished there. Ronnie Johnson of Chattanooga, TN, was third, followed by Freddy Smith of Kings Mountain, NC, and C.L. Pritchett of Cornelia, GA. The top five stayed the same for the entire 50 laps.

Fourteen of the 24 starters finished the race. Rounding out the top 10 were Clint Smith, Mike Duvall, Billy Clanton, Mike Head and Rex Ritchey.

Simmons was the only one of 27 drivers to qualify under 17 seconds in time trials, turning a lap of 16.98 seconds. Randy Rector and Jimmy Crawford were the only two local drivers to make the field. Rector won the consolation race and went out in a second-lap wreck.

Buck Simmons captured the NASCAR Busch All Star Super Series victory at Anderson Speedway July 1. (Don Coleman photo)

An article on the '86 race at Anderson Speedway, won by Simmons. According to Barry Wright, the hot driver at the time was Jeff Purvis. It was this race that Buck stopped Purvis' twelve race win streak. (Article provided by Bob Markos.)

Buck Simmons

By GENE PHILLIPS
Gaffney, SC 1987

GAFFNEY, SC (July 4) — Buck Simmons picked up $3,000 Saturday night, including a $1,000 bonus, for sweeping twin Late Model features at Cherokee Speedway.

The Baldwin, GA driver had an easy ride to the opening win as he led Mike Duvall, Butch Bowen, Hot Rod Lamance and Bill Morgan to the checkered flag.

Simmons had a more difficult time in the second race, though, as he had to start his Barry Wright/Marion Homes/Tri-City Drywall entry at the back of the pack.

His mount, powered by an RHS engine recently rebuilt by Clement Automotive, wasted little time in climbing to the front as Simmons followed Duvall to the head of the pack.

Duvall moved in front, but Simmons roared by on the backstretch

Buck Simmons won both Late Model features Saturday night at Cherokee. (Doug Phillips photo)

Sweeps Twin Cherokee LM Features

and pulled away for his second win of the evening.

Duvall finished second, followed by Lamance, Morgan and Dennis Williams.

Wally Fowler captured the Limited Sportsman feature to return to victory lane.

David Moyer finished second in the Charles Adams car as Wesley Johnson, David Smith and Roger Hamrick completed the top five.

Gaffney's Rick Adler took his second Street win of the season with a victory over Phil Ranson, Rusty Hamrick, Roger Melton and Todd Summey.

Buddy Lamb passed leader Linwood Fowler on the final lap to get the Thunder and Lightning win.

Fowler settled for second over Scottie Greene, Ronnie Sewell and Keith Fisher.

Tim Clayton took the Bomber race over Ricky Hines, Richard Smith, Joey Weller and Eddie Pack.

Buck takes two at Cherokee (SC) Speedway. (Article provided by Bob Markos.)

'90's. Buck won two Hav-A-Tampa races and one STARS Series event during that time. However, his lone STARS win was the 1990 Hillbilly 100 on September 2, 1990 at the Pennsboro Speedway (you can read about several of Simmons' wins at the end of this chapter).

Wright said, "One of the most hard luck finishes for us came at the 1990 Dirt Track World Championship at Pennsboro, West Virginia at the historic Pennsboro Speedway." Barry continued, "Buck had the fastest car all day. He started seventh, but had to come from the rear three times during

The only real threat to Buck Simmons' (41) lead in the Hillbilly 100 was lapped traffic on the half-mile clay oval. (Lauri A. Chandler photo)

Buck on his way to the checkered flag at the 1990 Hillbilly 100 in his #41 Barry Wright race car. (Photo from an article provided by Bob Markos.)

the 100 lap race." Barry finished by saying, "Buck caught the leader, Jack Boggs, with three laps to go and almost passed him for the win at the finish line."

After leaving the Barry Wright race car during the 1991 race season, Simmons drove for Wade Hegler in the Bert's Transmission white #41 race car. Hegler was one of the main executives for the Bert's Transmission dealerships in the South. Simmons and Hegler won a number of races together, they were especially hard to beat at the Cherokee Speedway. Buck also drove briefly for Morris Partain as the mid-'90's approached.

As I was leaving my interview at Barry Wright Race Cars in late January of 2017, Barry said, "Together Buck and I won around 200 races together. He was a tremendous racer who could actually win races on his own, just because he was good at adapting to the situation he was in." Wright continued, "Buck was easy on equipment, and was good at taking

Jack Boggs Pockets $50,000 in Pennsboro DTWC Win

By LAURI A. CHANDLER
Staff Writer

PENNSBORO, WV (Oct. 21) — "Black Jack" Boggs of Grayson, KY, pulled his 'Ace' from the hole to capture the checkers in the 10th annual STARS-sanctioned Dirt Track World Championship at the legendary Pennsboro Speedway.

The win was worth $50,000 to the two-time victor who had his mount towed after falling in a hole on the backstretch en route to the scales for post-race inspections. When his racer fell in the hole, it drowned his motor out, leaving him stranded on the backstretch. In victory lane, Boggs referred to the incident as a "little insurance at the scales."

The weight of Boggs's car satisfied track rules to ensure his victory.

"It's a super car," continued Boggs in victory lane. "I was running the car all out. The handling was a little off, but I knew I was going to give it my best shot. This kind of win feels good anytime!"

Boggs started from the second row outside and, after outside front row starter Scott Bloomquist experienced fuel pressure problems at the start, fell into second place behind fast qualifier Charlie Swartz.

Boggs rode Swartz' bumper for the first 45 laps while Billy Moyer worked his way through the top five to move around Boggs on lap 17. Three laps later, Moyer out-dragged Swartz down the backstretch and took the lead on lap 48. Moyer's lead, however dominant, was short-lived as on lap 65, the rearend broke loose, sending him in a spin over the third and fourth turn bank and out of contention.

Boggs then assumed the lead and held off charges by Larry Moore, who fell back with mechanical problems on the 74th lap, Bob Pierce, whose engine expired on lap 87, Freddy Smith and then Hillbilly 100 winner Buck Simmons, who moved underneath Smith on lap 97 and crossed the stripe on Boggs' rear quarter panel.

Following Boggs were Simmons, Smith, Swartz and Lynn Geisler.

Perhaps the quickest in the field was second-place finisher Simmons, who started in seventh and came from the rear three times before challenging Boggs for the lead in the final three circuits.

"The first tire we blistered, then we went out and had a flat," said Simmons of his tire problems. "I feel like we had the fastest car here."

According to Smith, tires were also a factor in his third-place finish. "During cautions the tires wouldn't turn. We started backing up, then the tires would come back in. Boggs was one of them deals, once you put on a set of tires, you can't change 'em."

There were 12 caution periods including one red flag stop for an accident involving defending race winner John Mason and Harold Redman. Mason bounced off the guardrail coming off turn two, and rolled head-on into Redman, who had nowhere to go. While both drivers were shaken up in the incident, the only reported injuries were a sore arm and stiff neck by Mason.

Ten of the 13 drivers still running at the finish were on the lead lap in the 100-lap event that was completed in one hour and 45 minutes.

One hundred and 17 drivers took time trials on Saturday with Swartz setting the fast pace at 20.82 seconds. Heats went to Eddie Carrier, Boggs, Bob Wearing Sr., Moore, Simmons and Smith. Donnie Moran captured the B main.

DTWC Feature Finish: 1. Jack Boggs, 100 laps, 2. Buck Simmons, 100, 3. Freddy Smith, 100, 4. Charles Swartz, 100, 5. Lynn Geisler, 100, 6. Eddie Carrier, 100, 7. B.J. Malott, 100, 8. Ron Davies, 100, 9. Gary Scaife, 100, 10. Paul Davis, 100, 11. Dale Mosier, 99, 12. Larry Moore, 99, 13. Mike Balzano, 98, 14. Mark Rinaldi, 95, 15. Rick Barton, 94, 16. Kenny Chrenshaw, 94, 17. Bob Pierce, 87, 18. Billy Moyer Jr., 64, 19. Steve Smith, 54, 20. Bruce Hordusky, 48, 21. Scott Bloomquist, 38, 22. John Mason, 30, 23. Harold Redman, 30, 24. Ronnie Johnson, 19, 25. Nathan Parkerson, 18, 26. John Gill, 17, 27. Bob Wearing Sr., 11.

Jack Boggs collected $50,000 and his second Dirt Track World Championship Sunday afternoon at Pennsboro Speedway. (Lauri A. Chandler photo)

With 117 drivers taking time trials, the field of drivers in the last chance race was as impressive as those in the main event. Donnie Moran secured his spot in the Dirt Track World Championship "A" feature by winning the comp. (Lauri A. Chandler photo)

Article on the 1990 Dirt Track World Championship. In this 100 lap race, Simmons came from the rear of the field three times, and still almost won the race at the finish. (Article provided by Bob Markos.)

an average running race car and somehow putting it in victory lane." In closing Wright said, "Simmons was something to watch in the '80's. During that time I don't believe there was no one better than Buck Simmons. He was a good friend and we never had a cross word between us the whole time we were together. Buck just lived to drive a race car."

Simmons at the Cherokee (SC) Speedway during the '92 season. Buck is in Wade Hegler's white #41. Hegler was in charge of the southern franchises of Bert's Transmission at the time. (Photo provided by Tony Hammett.)

Simmons Cops Governor's Cup at Volusia

1987

BARBERVILLE, FL (Jan. 3) — Georgia's Buck Simmons took advantage of a late-race opportunity Saturday night to pass polesitter Larry Moore and win the Florida State Governor's Cup Championship for Late Models at Volusia County Speedway.

Simmons had trailed Moore throughout the season-opening event and it appeared he would have to settle for second before misfortune struck the leader in the form of the lapped car of Florida's Tuck Trentham.

Moore, who earned the pole with a best lap of 19.376 seconds, and Simmons were running nose-to-tail into the first turn with five laps to go when the leader tangled with Trentham and Simmons drove past for the $4,000 victory.

"I was watching out for some of the other traffic and managed to get squeezed into the wrong spot," said Moore.

Following Simmons and Moore in the top five were Rob Underwood, Jack Boggs and Freddy Smith, while Wade Knowles, Billy Moyer Jr., Jack Pennington, Steve Shuman and Ed Gibbons completed the top 10.

Our Barry Wright Chassis and Hoosier tires were working just super all evening," said Simmons of the car's handling capabilities which allowed him to make his winning move when Moore got in trouble.

The first half of the race was slowed by cautions for some minor incidents and the most serious accident came on lap 67 when Trentham, Steve Moran and Rollie Alvers tangled to knock all three Floridians from contention.

Heat race winners were Boggs, Freddie Query, Knowles and Underwood. H.E. Vineyard captured the consolation win.

Zephyrhills' Mike Rudder overtook early leader Danny Bowman to win the Mini-Stock portion of the Governor's Cup Championships.

Ray Luechy, Don Ezell and Dave Wilson completed the top five in the four-cylinder competition.

Oxford's Bobby Peavy won the Cyclone feature and David Showers of St. Augustine was the Street Stock winner as the track opened its weekly racing for 1987.

Governor's Cup Finish: 1. Buck Simmons, 2. Larry Moore, 3. Rob Underwood, 4. Jack Boggs, 5. Freddy Smith, 6. Wade Knowles, 7. Billy Moyer, 8. Jack Pennington, 9. Steve Shuman, 10. Ed Gibbons, 11. Cecil Eunice, 12. Andy Knowles, 13. H.E. Vineyard, 14. John Yearsley, 15. Terry Mock, 16. Dennis Bennett, 17. Ronnie Johnson, 18. C.J. Rayburn, 19. Tuck Trentham, 20. Gene Evans, 21. Rollie Alvers, 22. Steve Moran, 23. Dick Potts, 24. Brian Mackey.

Buck Simmons (41) gets by leader Larry Moore (14) on his way to victory in the Florida Governor's Cup 100 at Volusia County Speedway January 3. (Mike Gibson photo)

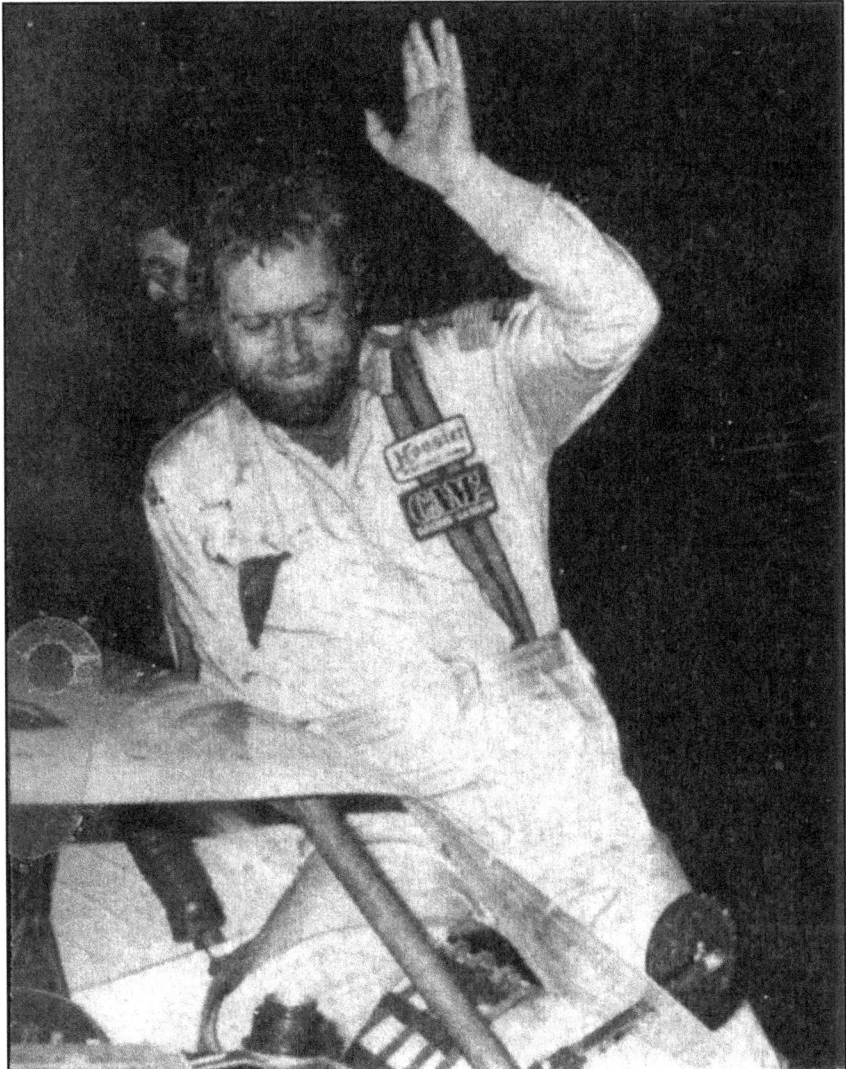

Buck Simmons emerges from his car after winning the Florida Governor's p 100 Late Model race at Volusia County January 3. (Mike Gibson photo)

Simmons Muscles to Victory in Metrolina Opener

By TRENT THOMASSON
Charlotte, NC *1987*

CHARLOTTE, NC (Mar. 15) — Buck Simmons muscled his way through the field Sunday to win the Late Model feature as Metrolina Speedway opened its season.

After moving to second by the halfway point, Simmons engaged leader Hank Jarman in a hotly contested battle on the newly renovated half-mile clay oval before an estimated crowd of 2,500 fans.

Simmons worked his way around Jarman on lap 20 and held off the early leader for the win.

Ed Gibbons placed third with Butch Bowen and Tim Moose completing the top five.

David Boggs, Steve Phillips, Kenneth Rominger, Freddie Query and Mike Anderson rounded out the top 10. Jarman and Stuart Taylor won the heats.

Ira Small collected the checkers in the Semi-Modified feature by holding off Lou Hardin and Garon Miller.

David Timmerman and Gene Anderson filled out the top five. Heats went to Neil Horne and Kenny Poiston.

Hobby division feature honors went to Doug Ghant over Buddy Crook, Johnny Arrants, Billy McConnell and Ricky Story.

The Sigmon brothers, Timmy and Kenny, staged a slam-bang affair that kept the fans on their feet throughout the Super Stock feature before Timmy took the checkers. Eddie Bearden, Tommy Smith and Randy Burris completed the top five.

Ray Hawk took the Enduro win, while Dawn Beaty claimed the Ladies feature.

Above, Buck Simmons (left) is congratulated by Metrolina promoter Doug Cooper after winning the Late Model opener. Below, Simmons (41) battles with Hank Jarman (555) in the March 15 event. (Randy Houser photos)

Buck Simmons Paces Wilson Harvest Festival 200

By JOY PERRY
Wilson, NC *1987*

WILSON, NC (Nov. 1) — Buck Simmons of Baldwin, GA, took the Tri-City Drywall/Barry Wright race car from flag to flag for 100 laps at Wilson County Speedway Sunday afternoon, claiming the $7,000 first place prize in the Harvest Festival 200 Late Model Stock feature.

After having the top 10 finishers of the dash-for-cash event inverted, Simmons started from the pole even though Freddy Smith actually had the fastest qualifying time of 21.72 seconds at the half-mile clay oval.

Simmons established quite a lead and was never seriously challenged after the wave of the green flag. Hank Edwards of Hope Mills brought the Pizza Hut TransAm to take second place, followed by the "the Flinstone Flyer" Mike Duvall of Gaffney, SC.

Jack Pennington arrived in time for the driver's meeting after competing in Woodstock, GA, to drive the Pipeline TransAm that had been qualified by Tom Usry. Pennington managed fourth place after the spoiler on the left side of the car broke, causing handling problems.

Loy Allen Jr. from Fuquay-Varina rounded out the top five in the Deacon Jones Pontiac.

The 100-lap event was slowed by six cautions with 28 cars taking the green and had the top 11 finishers on the lead lap at the fall of the checkered flag.

Favored Winston Cup competitor Rodney Combs was sidelined when his motor locked up, relegating him to a 16th place finish.

Harvest Festival 200 Late Model Finish: 1. Buck Simmons, 100 laps; 2. Hank Edwards, 100; 3. Mike Duvall, 100; 4. Jack Pennington, 100; 5. Loy Allen Jr., 100; 6. Kevin Rigsbee, 100; 7. Jimmy Kelley, 100; 8. Jimmy Hatchell, 100; 9. Steve Odom, 100; 10. Gary Allison, 100; 11. Hank Jarmon, 100; 12. Freddy Smith, 98; 13. Eddie Massengill, 96; 14. Mack Hyatt, 96; 15. Gary Mabe, 94; 16. Rodney Combs, 78; 17. Randy Thurman, 71; 18. Shelton McNair Jr., 61; 19. Jimmy Edwards Jr., 45; 20. Ray Mason, 36; 21. Frank Harrell Jr., 36; 22. Michael Mason, 30; 23. David Lucas, 54; 23. Randy Renfrow, 33; 24. Jimmy Neighbors, 26; 25. Milton Williamson, 32; 26. Roger Matthews, 10; 27. Bill Newby, 0.

Buck Simmons Takes $5,000 I-85 Prize

By JIM BLACKWELL
Greer, SC *1991*

GREER, SC (Mar. 9) — Buck Simmons captured the checkers in the Late Model main, winning $5,000 in the rain delayed event Saturday afternoon at I-85 Raceway. The race, originally scheduled for February 23, was delayed two weeks by inclement weather.

Simmons, starting from the pole in his Barry Wright/Cohen's Drywall mount, fell to second behind outside front row starter Ricky Weeks at the drop of the green.

On lap 10 following a restart Simmons took over the front spot. This pass proved to be worth $5,000 as he led the remaining 40 laps.

Following Simmons was Weeks, Daryl Key, Jerry Lark and Roger Hamrick.

Sportsman action saw Robert Bradley take the lead from pole starter John Gibson on lap three and lead until the checkers fell.

Bradley was followed by Mike Gault, Gibson, Wally Fowler and Earl Davis.

In the Limited Sportsman division, Eddie Pack moved underneath race-long leader Lynn Taylor on the white flag lap to take the win.

Pack was followed by Taylor, Gary Ramsey, Vic Owens and Bo Smith.

Modified Mini Stocks saw Mike Holcombe start from the pole and lead the entire race. Holcombe was followed by Ryan Owens, Bruce Absher, Billy Brown and Goob Waddell.

Third-place runner Glenn Holcombe took advantage of a tangle between the top two cars on the white flag lap to win the Mini Stock main. He was followed by Brian Bentley, Hoot McCall, Steve Matthews and Mike Billie.

The new Charger division saw David Thornton take the win over Truman Gillespie.

LM Feature Finish: 1. Buck Simmons, 2. Ricky Weeks, 3. Daryl Key, 4. Jerry Lark, 5. Roger Hamrick, 6. Jimmy Fowler, 7. Dennis Williams, 8. Garland Hobgood, 9. Wendell Taylor, 10. Tim Cooper, 11. Jimmy Taylor, 12. Jeff Moss, 13. Rooster Ghant, 14. Alan Poyner, 15. Tony Russell, 16. Kenny Lamb, 17. Blake Shewmaker, 18. Hugh Andrews, 19. Joe Littlejohn, 20. Donnie Smith, 21. Will Hobgood, 22. Buddy Wofford, 23. William Morgan, 24. Jerry Brown, 25. Dale Ball, 26. Marvin Trammell.

Buck Simmons Takes Sumter's LM Outlaw Win

By BONNIE COLE
Sumter, SC *1991*

SUMTER, SC (Mar. 30) — Buck Simmons of Augusta, GA won the Late Model Outlaw season opener Saturday night at Sumter Rebel Speedway.

Simmons, driving the MCE Racing/Roger Byers-wrenched/Barry Wright house car, started on the pole after posting the fastest qualifying time of 14.48. Lee Mintz started opposite Simmons with a 14.77. Simmons led from the start and was never threatened.

Mintz maintained his second position while Ed Gibbons, Dion Deason and Bob Sharp rounded out the top five.

Track promoter Bobby Sisson was enthusiastic about the Late Model Outlaw races scheduled for Sumter in the 1991 season.

"The Late Model car count was a little low, but the ones who were here are truly the best," Sisson said. "I never expected these guys to run as fast as they did tonight because of the rain we've had and the condition of the track. Next month's Outlaw race ought to be a real thriller and with twice as many cars."

Ronnie Johnson posted his first win in the Super Stock main event. Gerald Mintz won the right to the pole position with a qualifying time of 17.46. Tim Holladay started opposite Mintz with an 18.18.

Mintz took the early lead and Johnson began working his way to the front from his fifth starting position.

By the halfway mark, Johnson had advanced to the top spot and held it to the end. Mintz settled for second and Ruby McCoy finished third. Holladay and Tim Singletary rounded out the top five in fourth and fifth respectively.

In the Hobby division, Robbie Disher captured the win. Disher started on the second row behind polesitter Gene Stokes and George Scott but by the halfway point had taken the lead and held on for the win.

Scott finished in the second slot and Scott Dabbs came from the rear to finish third. Bob Powell placed fourth and Butch Tolson was fifth.

Kevin Hodge slated his first win in the Pure Stock division.

Hodge started on the second row and put immediate pressure on leader Lonnie Hodge. K. Hodge grabbed the lead in turn two just after the mid point of the race and L. Hodge dropped to the second spot.

In the last laps, L. Hodge spun but recovered in time to salvage his second place finish. Terry Anderson finished third follwed by Lane Viavoda and Roger Horne. L. Hodge received the Busch Hard Charger Award.

In the Gamecock Girls division, Karen Cooper took the checkered flag. Cooper finished first ahead of Rhonda Molina, Cheryl Roark and Jonette Thier.

Larry Brunnell finished first in the Mini Stock division. Brian Ingle placed second followed by Mike Elders, Allen Cook and Bubba Rucker.

Buck Simmons Beats Strong Cherokee LM Field

By LAURI A. CHANDLER
Staff Writer *1991*

GAFFNEY, SC (Apr. 28) — Buck Simmons of Baldwin, GA, out-dragged Scott Bloomquist for the lead on lap 28, then held off David Moyer by three car lengths for the win in the 50-lap, $3,000 to win, Late Model main event Sunday afternoon at Cherokee Speedway.

After Saturday night's washout of qualifying for the STARS-sanctioned Blue-Gray 100, the event was rescheduled for May 18-19.

"Scott took off and ran real good. When we got heat in the tires, mine started getting faster and faster. We got in some lapped traffic and I got by him," explained the veteran driver in victory lane.

"I hated that he blew an engine. I want to beat him, but not like that," said Simmons, who dedicated the win to his most devoted race fan and mother, Fay, on her birthday.

Simmons set fast time in qualifying with Bloomquist, Ed Gibbons and Jack Pennington earning the first four spots in time trials.

At the drop of the green, Bloomquist rocketed into the first turn and held a substantial lead over Simmons, Moyer, Freddy Smith and Mike Duvall.

A caution on the 12th lap tightened the field, but within three laps, Bloomquist had again widened the gap between himself and the field.

By the 20th circuit, Duvall maneuvered around Smith for fourth while Simmons began to close on the leader.

Without benefit of a caution, the leaders began working heavy traffic and on the 28th lap, Simmons out-dragged Bloomquist on the frontstretch for the lead.

Two laps later, on a caution restart, Bloomquist's engine went in a plume of smoke as he entered the first turn. Simmons led the remaining laps while Bob Pierce moved into the top five.

Following the Tri-City Dry Wall/Cohen's Dry Wall/Barry Wright racer across the stripe were Moyer, Duvall, Smith and Pierce. Completing the top 10 were Rodney Combs, Mike Balzano, John Mason, Hot Rod LaMance and Ron Davies.

There were six cautions during the event for minor spins and mechanical problems. Of the 26 starters, 15 were running at the finish.

Roger Hamrick scored the win in the Pepsi Limited Modified main, besting Jerry Lark, Dennis Williams, Will Hobgood and Wally Fowler. Joe Littlejohn and Hamrick won heats.

In the Thunder & Lightning division, Robert Bradley took the checkers over Danny Willis and Melvin Revis. Mitchell Duvall came from the rear of the field to finish fourth with Joe Earle rounding out the top five.

Bruce Absher captured the checkers in the Baby Bomber rump. Finishing behind were Phil LeCroy, Roger Pate, Todd Revis and Tim Lowery. Donnie Beason and Absher won heats.

In the Bomber main, Jeff Knight took yet another win, finishing ahead of Bo Mace, Barry Duncan, Benjie Whitesides and Chuck Pearson.

Tim Howard picked up the win in the Stock Fours, with Wayne Clayton, Steve McIntyre, Steve Melton and Jim Blackburn rounding out the top five.

LM Feature Finish: 1. Buck Simmons, 2. David Moyer, 3. Mike Duvall, 4. Freddy Smith, 5. Bob Pierce, 6. Rodney Combs, 7. Mike Balzano, 8. John Mason, 9. Hot Rod LaMance, 10. Ron Davies, 11. Jack Pennington, 12. Don Gross, 13. Tim Hitz, 14. Jack Boggs, 15. Chub Frank, 16. Rocky Hodges, 17. Dion Deason, 18. Todd Andrews, 19. Scott Bloomquist, 20. Ricky Weeks, 21. Hob Wearing Jr., 22. Doug Sanders, 23. Daryl Key, 24. Billy Scott, 25. Bob Cowen, 26. Ed Gibbons.

Buck Simmons celebrates his $3,000 Late Model win Sunday at Cherokee. (Randy Houser photo)

Buck Simmons receives his trophy at Lancaster from Hav-A-Tampa's Jimmy Mosteller. (Brian Patton photo)

Lancaster Hav-A-Tampa Run to Buck Simmons

By LARRY D. WILLIAMS
Lancaster, SC *1991*

LANCASTER, SC (May 2) — Buck Simmons led from flag to flag to claim the win and $3,000 in the Hav-A-Tampa Late Model qualifier at Lancaster Speedway Thursday night.

The checkered flag by Simmons, secured him a position in the Hav-A-Tampa Shootout, to be held September 27-28, at Dixie Speedway in Woodstock, GA.

In his Barry Wright Race Cars/Cohen's Drywall/Tri City Drywall Chevrolet, Simmons also topped the field in qualifying and set a new track record with a time of 19.73 seconds.

"It was all I could do to hold off Scott (Bloomquist) at the finish," said Simmons in victory lane. "My tires were wearing down due to the hardness of the track."

Bloomquist pulled alongside Simmons several times in the final laps of the race, but to no avail. Simmons was able to hold him off to the end.

The closeness of the race was reflected in the finish. When the checkers fell, the first three cars were nearly bumper to bumper when they crossed the line.

Dion Deason, starting ninth in the field, took third. He made a hard charge in the closing five laps to overtake Paul Croft on lap 45 of the 50-lapper.

Croft ran second for a third of the race and held the third spot until Deason moved in. Croft finished fourth with Rodney Combs rounding out the top five.

In other divisions, Will Hobgood, substituting for Rusty Robinson, took top honors in the Modified Six feature.

Hobgood was a solid winner, leading from start to finish. Perry Hobgood, Mike Huey, Todd Hammond and Randy Terry followed.

main, moving up from the rear of the field.

He inherited the lead from Darrell Cauthen when Cauthen encountered mechanical problems.

West challenged Cauthen several times before the early leader slowed.

Robbie Jordan, Rusty Broome, Brian Mahaffey and Allen Cunningham rounded out the top five. Randy Smith and Cauthen won heats.

Jeff Knight closed the evening, making it two for the season in the Street Stockers. Knight led from start to finish in the caution-filled event.

Ed Watkins, Wes Parrot, Lester Robinson and Dennis Knight, the winner's brother, rounded out the top five.

Gary Parker

Buck Simmons celebrates his Super Late Model win Saturday night at Cherokee. (Randy Houser photo)

Buck Simmons Blisters Cherokee Field

1992

GAFFNEY, SC (May 23) — Buck Simmons, the original "Georgia Bandit" proved to be too much for the Super Late Model field to handle Saturday night at Cherokee Speedway.

Simmons, in the Wa-Don Racing entry, checked out early in the feature and held off a hard-charging Billy Hicks to score his third win of the year on Cherokee's half-mile.

Hicks had his best run of the year to claim second place. Doug Sanders made a late move to take third from Paul Croft. Jimmy Fowler came across the stripe fifth.

Linwood Fowler visited victory lane in the Thunder & Lightning race for his first win of the year at the track. Fowler survived a protest from runner-up Tim Goode to take the top prize.

Mitch Duvall came in third with Melvin Revis fourth and Andy Bennett fifth.

The Baby Bomber feature was won by Bruce Absher. The win was his first of the year at Cherokee. Michael Cogdell took second, Turkey Craig was third, Dale Petty fourth and Dennis Franklin took fifth.

Rodney Goins scored the Bomber victory. Max Doggett finished a close second. Finishing third through fifth in order were Phil Johnson, Lewis Clayton and Danny Ledford.

Jim Blackburn was back in victory lane in the Stock Four race that started 30 cars. Second through fifth were Ken Sides, David Hawkins, Ricky Rogers and Charles Byars.

The Pure Stock race was taken by Perry Waters. Chad Tessnear was second, Howard Hill third, James Hill fourth and David Echols fifth.

Buck Simmons Tops Thunder Valley Run

LAWNDALE, NC (Sept. 25) — Buck Simmons notched the Late Model victory Friday night at Thunder Valley Speedway.

Following Simmons across the stripe were Ricky Weeks, Buddy Smith, Lee Mintz and Doug Sanders.

Mike Gault took the Thunder and Lightning win over Tim Clayton, Eric Rogers, Bobby Howard and Donnie Price.

In Super Modified Four action, Ronnie Sewell took top honors with Larry Hoyle, Jeff Hastins, Ron Parker and Shane Absher following.

Gary Travis scored the Modified Four Baby Bomber feature. Finishing second through fifth were Tim Smith, Robert Bradley, Joe Dupuis and Rick Story.

Michael Brock drove to the Bomber checkers. Keith Tate took second, David Crawford third, Dale Chapman fourth and Shann Cook fifth.

In the Super Stock Four feature, Paul Payne Jr., took the win with Brent McNeeley, Doug Hastings, Scott Lail and Ron Hensley rounding out the top five.

Mark Blackwell drove to the Stock Four win. Completing the first five finishers were Jim Blackwell, Dale Brown, Kenny Tessneer and Bill Towery.

Chapter Seven
RACING CLOSER TO HOME

After racing dirt late models and outlaw wedge race cars nationally for legendary race car builder Barry Wright for years; Buck was back at his Baldwin, Georgia home in early 1997 about ready to retire from the sport he loved. According to Wright, "Buck drove for me on three separate occasions over about a ten year period. During that time he won between 175 and 200 races driving my cars."

Now at over 50 years of age and in poor health, Hall of Fame driver, Buck Simmons was through with racing on the national scene. Simmons felt that with his wins total close to 1000, and his many racing accomplishments; he had nothing else to prove to the racing world.

In early 1997 several people played a key roll in bringing Simmons back to the racing scene. Those people included Shane Worley, Gerald Voyles, Bruce Taylor, Tim Simmons, and Slab Sellers.

That year Shane Worley approached Buck with a racing plan. In the end, Shane brought Simmons out of retirement with the promise of racing only on the local scene. Worley put Buck in the blue and white Worley Monument race car.

Buck's return to dirt late model racing was a victorious one. Right out of the gate, Simmons won six races in a row at Lavonia (GA) Speedway, resulting in the track promoter putting a "bounty" on Buck. This brought several racing stars to Lavonia to try and collect that bounty. Among those drivers were, Mike Duvall, Hot Rod LaMance, Jack Pennington, Casey Roberts, and others. At one point, because of a dispute with Lavonia's track officials, Simmons went to Toccoa (GA) Speedway and scored a win on a night he was supposed to be at Lavonia defending his win streak.

Buck Simmons takes the win at Toccoa Raceway in the Worley Monument Company #01. At the time, Simmons had a bounty on him in this race car at the Lavonia (GA) speedway. (Photo provided by Tim Simmons.)

Later that year, the Simmons/Worley race team traveled to the historic Dixie Speedway in Woodstock, Georgia; the sight of a number of Buck's early career late model wins. From the beginning, Simmons was against the trip. Buck started 12th in that race. After using all of his years of racing experience, Simmons drove through the field. In a thrilling finish, reminisce of one of those classic early '70's Dixie races, Buck finished second missing the win by a mere two feet. After the race an angry Simmons said, "See I told you we had no business coming down here." According to some, this eventually led to a parting of the ways between Simmons and Worley.

It was not long before Buck made the first of his two driving stints for Carnesville, Georgia's Gerald Voyles in the Voyles Auto Sales red #41 race car. The team won races at 106 (GA) Speedway, Lavonia (GA) Speedway, and Toccoa (GA) Raceway. Voyles said, "A number of business interests was one of the contributing factors to the race team ending before the '99 season."

Simmons powers thru a turn in his famous power slide in the Gerald Voyles Auto Sales red #41. This was during Buck's first stint as the driver of the Voyles' race car. (Photo provided by Gerald Voyles.)

The '99 racing season saw Simmons return to the Shane Worley race team. This time the race team couldn't return to their '97 racing magic. Buck's only win for Worley that year came at Whittier, North Carolina's Smoky Mountain Speedway. However, the race proved to be a memorable one, as Simmons set a new track qualifying record (a record that stood until the track closed in 2005). Then Buck went on to give the race fans and the promoter a racing show, as he led every lap of the feature race.

Simmons also briefly drove for Slab Sellers in '99. Their only victory together proved to be another memorable win. Buck took the checkered flag at Westminister (SC)

Buck takes the checkered flag at Whittier, North Carolina's Smoky Mountain Speedway, driving the Shane Worley/Simmons Electric #41. (Photo provided by Tim Simmons.)

Speedway in the $5,000 to win "South Carolina State Championship" race. A number of people have said this was the last big money win of Simmons' racing career.

Buck Simmons takes the win at Westminister (SC) Speedway in a $5,000 to win race in 1999. This proved to be Buck's only win for the Slab Sellers race team. (Photo provided by Tim Simmons.)

The spoils of victory. Simmons wins a feature race at 106 (GA) Speedway in 2000. Tim Simmons waves the checkered flag, as set-up man Bruce Taylor looks on from behind the Walter Newman #41 race car. (An Ed Rogers photo provided by Tim Simmons.)

2000 proved to be a great year for Buck. Bruce Taylor, one of the region's best race chassis set-up men; and Tim Simmons of Baldwin, Georgia's Simmons Electric Company joined forces with Buck. Taylor knew that Simmons still had the desire and racing skills necessary to win races. Earlier, Taylor had beaten Simmons for the 1998 Lavonia Speedway points championship. During that championship chase, Taylor saw firsthand how tough Buck still was in a race car.

By this time, Taylor had accomplished his racing goals as a driver; but still wanted to be involved in racing. So it came as no surprise that Bruce Taylor, his dad James, and Tim Simmons would put the legendary Simmons in their race car.

Together this Walter Newman red #41 race car scored twelve checkered flags for this newly formed race team. At times during the 2000 race season, "ole" Buck looked like the driver of old. On several occasions Simmons battled some of the region's best dirt stars for his wins at 106 Speedway, Lavonia, and other tracks.

Finally, Tim Simmons told me about a memorable race night at the 106 Speedway. Tim said, "Buck had won the feature race in our car. He then got in Tim King's #85 race car (one normally driven by Hot Rod LaMance) and won a second feature race." Then a smiling Tim said, "As if that was not enough he decided to drive a four cylinder in their feature race. Buck finished second, losing by a half a car length at the finish line to Clayton Turner. In closing Tim said, "Buck got confused on the amount of laps left in the race or he would have won three feature races in one night."

As the 2000 racing season came to an end, Simmons was standing ever closer to his 1000th feature win. In 2001 Simmons planned to return to the Gerald Voyles race car, and the quest for his 1000th career win.

Buck scores another win for the Bruce Taylor/Walter Newman/Simmons Electric race team. From left to right are James Taylor (Bruce's dad), Tina Simmons, Tim Simmons, Anthony Wall, Jonathan Taylor, Buck Simmons, and Bruce Taylor. (Photo provided by Tim Simmons.)

Chapter Eight
THE SIMMONS/VOYLES RACE TEAM: THE CHASE FOR 1000 WINS

After fifty years of hard racing and hard living, Buck Simmons found himself with 981 feature wins and a career that appeared to be over. It looked like that elusive 1000th win was not to be. But as the old saying goes, "Help was on the way."

Carnesville, Georgia businessman, Gerald Voyles again came to the rescue. Simmons had first teamed with Voyles in '97 in the Voyles Auto Sales red #41 race car.

Buck Simmons in the Voyles Auto Sales #41 in 1997. (Photo provided by Gerald Voyles.)

Like many others, Voyles knew that Buck's win total was accurate. Simmons' mom, Faye, had always kept a record of all of her son's races from the beginning of his career. Knowing that Simmons needed only nineteen more wins to reach a 1000 wins; Voyles agreed to a plan to help Buck achieve that goal. Gerald said, "The timing was right for both of us. We both wanted to continue to race; but neither of us wanted to run the roads anymore, me as a car owner and him as a driver."

So, in 2001 Simmons teamed with the last car owner he would ever drive for, Gerald Voyles. That year they unveiled the John Deere green #41 race car. The year ended with Simmons' win total at 997.

The Gerald Voyles Equipment Company John Deere green #41 (Photo by Tony Hammett.)

However, the 2002 race season would prove to be "one for the ages" for Simmons and his John Deere race team. Bruce Taylor was added to the team as the set-up man for the #41. The team again raced locally at, Hartwell, Lavonia, Toccoa, Cherokee, Tri-County, Westminister. They even traveled to the historic Dixie Speedway and East Alabama Motor Speedway on a couple of occasions..It was a Friday night in early April 2002 and Simmons was at Carnesville's 106 Speedway in search of win number 998. The newspaper sports reporters were there, including the Atlanta Journal-Constitution sports reporter, Rick Minter. An Athens television station was also on hand to watch the legendary Buck Simmons inch closer to his 1000th win.

All the focus was on Buck and he responded with a great practice session. However, Simmons had a poor qualifying run and was starting seventh. This was not where he wanted to be on a night when all eyes were focused on him.

Usually when you qualify that far back, that's where you normally finish. But this is the "Living Legend" we are talking about here.

The crowd of about 700 race fans saw the flagman wave the green for the start of a 30 lap feature. Simmons wasted no time in moving past the sixth place car and into fifth position. A buzz started sweeping through the crowd as Buck moved quickly to fourth. With four laps remaining, Simmons found himself behind only the 24 year old Casey Roberts in his #101 race car. There were only three laps remaining when Bucks years of driving experience took over. As the cars came by the flag stand, Simmons drove to the bottom and passed Roberts. The big crowd came to its feet and went wild as Buck pulled away in the final laps for the win.

In victory lane a relieved Simmons said, "It took all my 42 years of driving experience to win that one."

Recently I talked with legendary race reporter/writer Rick Minter. Rick said, "I asked Buck how he was able to win that race in such exciting fashion." Simmons just smiled that old Buck smile and said, "I was not going to let all you people in the press and TV down. So I pulled all my experience out to win this one for you guys and the race fans."

Buck Simmons in victory lane after a win at 106 Speedway in Carnesville, GA. That is Voyles' grandson, Adam Smith, holding the checkered flag. (Photo provided by Gerald Voyles.)

Simmons quickly won the next race and the stage was set for his historic 1000th win on May 11, 2002 at Lavonia (GA) Speedway.

As race fans, the media, and a few television stations drove through the small Northeast town of Lavonia, Georgia; one got the feeling that this was no ordinary race night at Lavonia Speedway. All eyes were on a dirt late model driver named Buck Simmons, known to many as just, "The living legend."

The scene was now set for Simmons to try and win his 1000th feature race. It was a packed house at promoter Mike White's Lavonia Speedway as the cars were ready to qualify for the night's events. The crowd was on its feet as Simmons, in his Voyles racing John Deere green #41, hit the track to qualify. As had happened on so many occasions during his legendary career; old Buck was on the pole for the start of the super late model feature.

An excited overflow crowd was on its feet as the green flag waved for the start of the race. Simmons jumped to the lead and raced an almost flawless race. There might as well have been no bleachers at the track that night; because hardly anyone sat down the entire race.

As the laps wound down, you could feel the excitement in the air as the white flag waved on Simmons and the rest of the field. When Simmons came out of the fourth turn for the final time going toward the checkered flag; the big crowd, and even many of the drivers, erupted in a wild celebration for Buck Simmons. He had done it! Buck had scored his 1000th win (read about this race in a fine article by Brian McLeod at the end of this chapter).

Simmons powers thru turn four at the Lavonia (GA) Speedway. Buck scored his 1000th win there on May 11, 2002. (Photo provided by Tony Hammett.)

After the race in victory lane an almost speechless Simmons said, "Boy am I glad that is over." Hundreds of race fans and the media gathered around Simmons and took pictures and wished him well. Even car owner Gerald Voyles was glad it was over. Voyles said, "It was one of the most rewarding things that I have been a part of in racing." He continued, "It was a long time in coming. We hoped to get this win last year, but had some bad luck toward the end of 2001, and it just didn't happen then."

Later, Simmons was asked about his racing future. Buck told the big crowd and the media, "I have no plans to quite racing as long as I feel I am competitive. We'll just have to wait and see. I can now go back to enjoying racing without all the pressures of the last few months."

The 2002 racing season turned out to be one of the best in a long time for Simmons. A short time after his milestone win, Buck took the checkered flag for number 1,001 at 106 Speedway; and the very next night scored 1,002 on Saturday at Lavonia. He won No.1005 on June 8, 2002; and went on to score the last of his 1,012 wins at Toccoa (GA) Raceway in '03. In 2003 Buck climbed out of his legendary #41 for the last time, having won the last 31 races of his career in the Gerald Voyles' John Deere green race car.

During the last few years of his racing career, even Charles LeRoy "Buck" Simmons had to agree with his many race fans and family members. He was "The Living Legend."

Buck scores another win at 106 Speedway on his way to 1012 career wins. That is Janice and Gerald Voyles with Simmons in victory lane. (Photo provided by Gerald Voyles.)

It Dawned on Me by Brian McLeod

With 1,000th win, Simmons enjoys 'big moment'

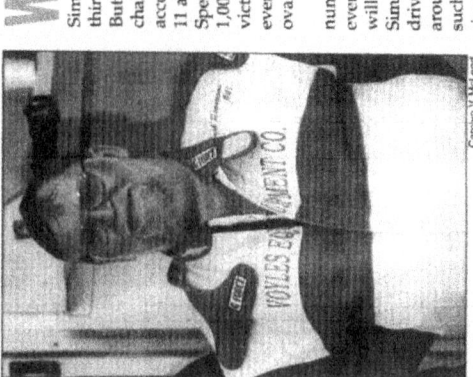

Buck Simmons of Baldwin, Ga., notched his 1,000th career feature victory May 11.
Carolyn V. McLeod

When you've reached as many milestones in your career as Baldwin, Ga., driver Buck Simmons has surpassed, you might think there's little left to accomplish. But the veteran driver chalked up another accomplishment May 11 at Lavonia (Ga.) Speedway, claiming his 1,000th career feature victory in a weekly event at the 3/8-mile oval.

That's a significant number, as nearly everyone in the sport will tell you. It puts Simmons among a very elite group of drivers, because few short track racers around the country can lay claim to such an impressive collection of victories. And the sport's records have always been sketchy, leaving some doubts about who has done it and who might be close.

But Simmons, one of dirt racing's superstars who helped put the sport on the national map with his involvement (and 1981 championship) on Robert Smawley's National Dirt Racing Association circuit, has been closing on the magic number for a few seasons now.

He hooked up with long-time car owner Gerald Voyles for an assault on the milestone, and has been a regular at Lavonia for about five seasons now. And like poetic justice, that's where the long-awaited victory occurred. And when the race announcer exited the press tower to do a trackside interview, he found a near-speechless Simmons awaiting on the frontstretch, according to track owner Mike White.

> "The fans were standing at the fence and cheering like crazy, and it was really a big moment."
>
> — Mike White, Lavonia (Ga.) Speedway promoter

"They said he was so excited he couldn't even talk," White said. "The fans were standing at the fence and cheering like crazy, and it was really a big moment. I'm glad it happened at our track, because he's been running here pretty regular for a few seasons. And that's certainly a big honor, to win that many races in your career."

White should know. He's a former racer, and remembers going to the tracks when he was younger and watching Simmons. And now that he's on the promotional side of the fence, he found himself watching him again, albeit from a different perspective.

"I used to pull for him when I was going to watch races," White said. "And he told me he really wanted to win his 1,000th race at our track, so I

Gary Parker

It Dawned on Me

continued from page 4

guess I was pullin' for him again! I also raced against him when I was running, so it's pretty important to me to have it happen at Lavonia. We're gonna take the checkered flag and get it embroidered for him, and I plan to have a plaque made to present to him in front of the fans. He deserves it."

Simmons was fast qualifier and led every lap at the semibanked oval. And just in case you're wondering, Simmons ain't stopping at 1,000. No sir. There are no thoughts of retirement just yet, at least from what he told the fans.

"He told the crowd that he was kinda glad it was over," White said. "He said there was a lot of pressure on him to get it done, especially last year because people were expecting it to happen. But he struggled a little, but now he's got a better car and it looks like he's gonna have a great season.

And he said he's gonna have fun now, cause he can sit back, relax and whatever happens is fine — just go racin' and with less pressure on him. And he said he'll probably race as long as his health and sponsorship will allow him. In fact, he's changing over to Ford and the team has a new GRT that they just brought back from Arkansas. So he ain't planning to quit just yet."

That's good news for dirt fans,

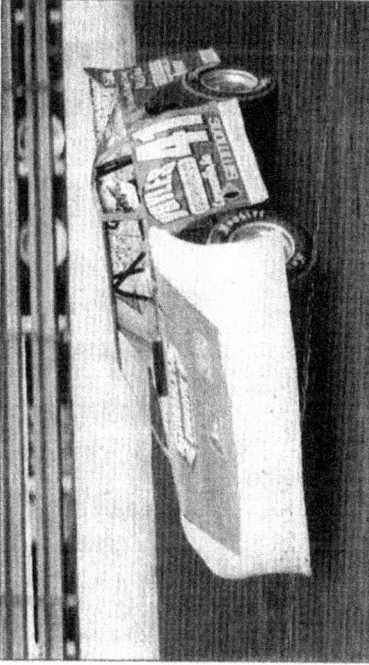

Buck Simmons was in his prime when he won the 1981 National Dirt Racing Association title, and he's still knocking victories off at weekly events.

because Simmons is a major part of a sport that's advanced from gritty backyard ovals to short track racing's mainstream. Dirt Late Model racing is a more respected segment of the sport than it was more than two decades ago, and Simmons was one of the men who helped usher the sport to its current status.

He raced against regional superstars such as Bud Lunsford, Doug Kenimer, Leon Archer, Charlie Hughes and Leon Sells, and also took his show on the road against the country's best with the NDRA. He was a teammate to fellow legend Larry Moore in Jim Erpowned machines with sponsorship from Tri-City Aluminum, driving that car to the NDRA title with 13 victories in 19 events. All totaled, he won 23 NDRA events.

Less well known is the fact that he dabbled in NASCAR Winston Cup Series competition, or that he was also a dominant driver on pavement. He raced with much success at Dixie (Ga.) Speedway during the short stretch that it was an asphalt oval, and his name appears among the top finishers in several editions of the prestigious Snowball Derby at Five Flags (Fla.) Speedway.

But no matter what he's done — or hasn't done — dirt racing will always remember Simmons for his 1,000th victory, which occurred rather appropriately on a red clay track that's tucked neatly away on a two-lane country road in Georgia. Simmons has traveled countless roads just like that one to ply his trade across the country, spending most of the years of his life in search of the perfect powerslide.

Chassis builders will tell you he's got a near-perfect feel for a race car, a gift that few drivers truly have. Simmons and famed Cowpens, S.C., car builder Barry Wright have spent a lot of time racing together, and Wright will tell you that if you get a car in the ballpark on chassis setup, Buck'll do the rest.

And Wright has to be correct, because we all know that Simmons has proved that theory before ... at least 1,000 times. NDD

Brian McLeod's 1000th win article.

Chapter Nine
BUCK'S TWO FAVORITE WINS

In his over forty years competing in the dirt late model ranks, Buck Simmons scored an amazing 1,012 feature wins, most of those in the dirt late models. Having watched Simmons race these cars since the early '70's, I think two of Simmons' checkered flags could be called his signature career wins.

The first of these wins occurred on October 13, 1985. The race would prove to be Robert Smawley and his NDRA series' last big event. The race was the second invitational race on the National Dirt Racing Association tour. The other was held at Smoky Mountain Speedway on September 23, 1984, with Tom Helfrich taking the win. Drivers representing tracks from all over the country were invited to compete in the $250,000 race known as the NDRA/Strohs Invitational held at the Kingsport (TN) Speedway.

Simmons came into the race with momentum on his side, having won the $10,000 Dutch Treats fast qualifier award the night before over a field of around 140 race cars. The money came from one of Smawley's newest sponsors, the Dutch Treats Cigar Company, who came on board with a $500,000 package for his series.

As the 100 lap race took the green flag, Buck Simmons, representing the I-85 Speedway in Greer, South Carolina, took the lead; a lead he would maintain for the entire race. According to Buck the race was not as easy a win as it sounds.

Also Earns $10,000 Dutch Treats Pole

Buck Simmons Earns 'Big Bucks' in NDRA/Stroh's Invitational

By NELSON REDD
Oxford, OH

KINGSPORT, TN (Oct. 13) — "I was under pressure from the first lap to the last lap, more pressure the last 10," said a weathier Buck Simmons after taking home the "big bucks" from the second annual NDRA/Stroh's $250,000 Invitational at New Kingsport Speedway Sunday afternoon.

When Simmons headed back to Baldwin, GA, Sunday night, NDRA officials had written his name on two checks — one for $20,000 following his flag-to-flag invitational victory, and another for $10,000 after the out-qualified 140 other drivers to win the Dutch Treats Pole Award night.

"The whole deal was when we qualified good," Simmons said. "That won the race for us."

Representing I-85 Raceway in Greer, SC, Simmons' victory also secured a $30,000 points fund for the track from the Stroh Brewery Company and NDRA.

"It was a helluva day," said Simmons as he capped off a perfect weekend, making his first start of the year in the Griffin Radiator/RHS Engines/Barry Wright stockappearing house car.

By virtue of his fast time, Simmons started the 100-lap feature on the pole. The start of the race was unlike any all weekend, as all 24 cars completed the first lap without incident. Simmons moved quickly to the point, with second-fast qualifier Tommy Joe Pauschert tucking in behind, followed by Larry Phillips, Billy Moyer and Willy Kraft.

The top five was shuffled early in the race when Kraft dropped Moyer to fifth on the second lap. Jeff Purvis settled into the top five one lap later.

Moyer settled into sixth, followed by Bob Pierce, Freddy Smith, Leon Sells and Scott Bloomquist. The top 10 remained the same for the first half of the race, with the drivers unable to find an opening to improve their position. Kenny Brightbill appeared to be the only driver able to run high on the tight 3/8-mile oval. He moved into 11th on lap 26 and joined the lead pack. The first 50 laps were uneventful, with only two cautions for minor incidents to slow the pace.

The action picked up in the second half of the race. Smith moved into seventh on lap 52 when a pushrod came through the valve cover of Pierce's engine. The resulting loss of power off the turns forced Pierce to change his line and he lost only one position.

Meanwhile, Simmons and Pauschert had opened a two-second lead over Kraft and Purvis. By the 72nd lap, the four cars had pulled together in a tight pack, and it looked like the first significant action was about to develop. As the quartet came off turn four tightly bunched, Pauschert made his move. Simmons shut the door and the third of six yellow flags appeared.

"I thought we could win about lap 65," Pauschert explained later. "The caution helped Buck."

Tire wear had become a factor at that point, with all the frontrunners' right rear rubber looking like asphalt slicks.

From that point, Simmons and

Buck Simmons glides through the turns at New Kingsport Speedway on his way to victory in the NDRA/Stroh's Invitational. (Brian Patton photo)

Pauschert settled into the bottom groove with the only significant changes in position coming from third on back.

Purvis grabbed third on lap 84 when Kraft began to quickly fade. Smith followed into fourth. They stayed that way until the finish. Bloomquist, completed the top five, moving into fifth with just three laps remaining.

Pierce, Sells, Phillips, Brightbill and Stan Massey rounded out the top 10.

The car Simmons drove to victory had a two-year-old Barry Wright chassis, with a new rear suspension.

"I think that's what made it feel good. It's two years old," Simmons said.

The top three qualifiers — Simmons, Pauschert and Moyer — were locked into the 24-car starting grid. Phillips, Purvis, Kraft, Pierce, Smith and Sells claimed heat victories Saturday night. Three starters were taken from each of the six heat races. The top three finishers from the consolation ran completed the starting grid, with Charles Powell III winning the 25-lap consolation race.

NDRA/Stroh's Invitational Finish: 1. Buck Simmons, 100. 2. Joe Pauschert, 100. 3. Jeff Purvis, 100. 4. Freddy Smith, 100. 5. Scott Bloomquist, 100. 6. Bob Pierce, 100. 7. Leon Sells, 100. 8. Larry Phillips, 100. 9. Kenny Brightbill, 100. 10. Stan Massey, 100. 11. Charles Powell III, 100. 12. Ronnie Johnson, 100. 13. Bobby Thomas, 100. 14. Willy Kraft, 100. 15. Ricky Williams, 100. 16. Robert Powell, 100. 17. Rex Richey, 100. 18. Billy Moyer, 99. 19. Rick Aukland, 88. 20. Gene Chupp, 75. 21. Mike Balzano, 78. 22. Rodney Combs, 39. 23. Don Swearengen, 22. 24. Tom Hearst, 4.

Buck Simmons accepts his $10,000 Dutch Treats Pole Award after setting the fastest time for the NDRA/Stroh's Invitational. (David Kocher photo)

He said, "I was under constant pressure from the first lap to the last. I had a lot more pressure on me the last 10 laps." That pretty much summed up the event. After the 24 starters completed the first lap without a caution; something that had not been done in the night's other races, the top 10 settled in for the first half of the race. The first half top 10 were, Simmons, followed by Tommy Lee Pauschert, Larry Phillips, Willy Kraft, Jeff Purvis, Billy Moyer, Bob Pierce, Freddy Smith, Leon Sells, and Scott Bloomquist.

The second half of the race saw Simmons and Pauschert open up about a two-second lead over the third and fourth place cars of, Kraft and Purvis. However, by lap 72, it appeared the Pauschert was going to make a move to pass Buck, but a caution flag put an end to that threat. Later, in a post race interview Pauschert said, "That caution helped Buck and probably won the race for him."

Simmons drove a two year old Barry Wright race car, with a new rear suspension system, to the victory and the winner's share of $20,000. The final top ten finishers were, Simmons, Pauschert, Purvis, Smith, Bloomquist, Pierce, Sells, Phillips, Brightbill, and Stan Massey in that order. In the end, Buck took home to Baldwin, Georgia a total of $30,000 in winnings in what he called, "A helluva day."

The second of his two signature wins took place in the late Summer of 1990.

It was Sunday, September 2, 1990, and the Labor Day weekend was upon the race fans and drivers at Pennsboro, West Virginia. It was only minutes before the start of the 22nd annual "Hillbilly 100." The STARS sanctioned race had brought 36 of its racing members to the event. In all, a total of 64 race cars had qualified, trying to make the 24 car field who would start the race. Charlie Swartz was the fastest qualifier at 21.15. He was followed by "Little" Ed Gibbons with

Buck Simmons captured his first-ever Hillbilly 100 victory in the 22nd annual STARS-sanctioned event. The win was worth $11,000 to the Baldwin, GA Late Model driver. (Lauri A. Chandler photo)

a time of 21.72. However, it would be Baldwin, Georgia's Buck Simmons who would start on the pole. He won that honor by winning the fast car dash.

As the cars came down the front straight-a-way to take the green; it was Simmons who jumped into the lead, using his famous power slide thru turns one and two. He pulled Steve Francis, Charlie Swartz, Ron Davies, and Ed Gibbons down the backstretch. The race stayed this way until lap 22, when Swartz moved to second past Gibbons as Francis took third.

As the crossed flags waved at the half way point, the fans were on their feet as Rodney Franklin, now probably the fastest car in the field, moved from his seventh starting position to pass second place Charlie Swartz. Swartz held the third position until a charging Donnie Moran powered by him in the closing 10 laps. After the race Swartz said, "A problem with my brakes probably cost me a chance at the win."

Buck Simmons took the checkered flag in his Tri-City Drywall/Cohen's Dry Wall/Hoosier/Barry Wright race car followed by, a hard charging Rodney Franklin, Donnie Moran, Charlie Swartz, and Mike Balzano (STARS points leader at the time) rounding out the top 5. The rest of the top 10 included, Steve Francis, Ed Gibbons, Bob Pierce, Scott Bloomquist, and Randy Boggs.

In victory lane a happy Simmons said, "I had a vibration in the car with a few laps to go. I was a little worried because I didn't know what it was. Other than that, the car ran perfectly all day." After being presented with the $11,000 winners check, a still smiling Buck said, "I am very pleased to win this race. When you outrun a field of this caliber you've done something."

I recently talked to his cousin, Tim Simmons about the two races. Tim said, "Buck always talked a lot about these two wins. For some reason he always was the most proud of his Hillbilly win." Tim continued, "I never could understand that, because there were more drivers at the Kingsport race. He also, had a bigger number of articles on the Kingsport race. Those included, articles in STOCK CAR RACING, with a cover photo." In closing he said, "Buck also won more money at the Kingsport race. He won $30,000 in all for the Kingsport win and $11,000 for the 1990 Hillbilly 100."

In the end it appears Buck thought more of his Hillbilly 100 win than his big NDRA win at Kingsport. However, a number of drivers in the sport would have loved to be in Buck's shoes. Many a driver would have given their racing careers for just one of those wins.

Buck Simmons (41) powers his MCE Racing/Tri City Dry Wall/Cohen's Dry Wall/MDcals racer to a flag to flag victory in the Hillbilly 100. (Lauri A. Chandler photo)

Here's Buck after his win in the 1990 Hillbilly 100, his all-time favorite dirt late model win. (Photo by Lauri A. Chandler.)

Chapter Ten
SOME FINAL THOUGHTS ON THE LIVING LEGEND

Charles Leroy Simmons, just "Buck" Simmons to the racing world, was one of those kids who knew early on what he wanted to do in life. By the time he was twelve years old, sitting on a box to see over the steering wheel of a car, his mind was set on a career in racing.

When most kids were out playing baseball, football, and other sports; Buck was driving the water truck at Tommy Irvin's Banks County (GA) Speedway. By fourteen Simmons was racing jalopies at Banks County Speedway, Athens Speedway, and other tracks in the area. When he was fifteen he was racing and winning in the modified ranks against some of the best drivers in the South. Drivers like Tootle Estes, Bud Lunsford, Cabbage Pendley, Bill York, and others.

A couple of years later, he was competing in the popular modified skeeter ranks in both, Georgia and South Carolina. Driving for some of the best modified car builders in the business like, James "Jabo" Bradberry and Harold "Speedy" Evans. Again, he continued his winning ways against some of the best mudslingers the sport had to offer.

By the time he was in his early twenties, Simmons had a win total approaching 200 wins; more than most of the older drivers he was competing against.

Buck Simmons standing beside his modified race car. (Photo provided by J.R. Whitt.)

The dawn of the late '60's saw Buck move to the "new kid on the block," dirt late models. Beginning with car owners Harold "Speedy" Evans and J.R. Whitt, Simmons showed no signs slowing down when it came to taking checkered flags. He raced at Hartwell, Athens, and other tracks in the Northeast Georgia, and South Carolina areas.

Simmons at Hartwell (GA) Speedway in the Da-Je Homes/Harold "Speedy" Evans #41 Chevelle. Hartwell allowed the late models to run wings on the top. (Photo provided by Bob Markos.)

In 1969 he traveled South to Woodstock, Ga. and a new dirt racing facility known as Dixie Speedway. That first year at Dixie his true racing talent was on display for the racing world to see; as he won 18 of the 22 races held that year out-dueling some of the best drivers in the South. That my friends is call almost total domination!

It was in 1970 that I got my first glimpse of Simmons in a dirt late model at Dixie speedway. I was a member of Jody Ridley's pit crew and we came down for the opening race that year. We had been hearing about this driver from the Metro Atlanta area called Buck Simmons. We were accustom to winning about everywhere we raced at the time, so we expected to come down and continue our winning ways.

With qualifying over we were starting outside of Simmons on the front row. Jody's brother, Biddle, and I walked over between turns one and two to watch the cars come through. The green flag waved and Buck jumped to the lead, going into turns one and two he put the DaJe Homes, black and gold #41 into his famous power slide and coming out of two, he pulled Jody, in the #98 blue Ford Fairlane, about ten car lengths going down the back straight-a-way. Biddle and I looked at one another with our jaws dropped and said, "Wow!"

Simmons continued his winning ways during the '70's driving for Evans and Whitt, Max Simpson, Tommy Hickman, and Jimmy Thomas in the revolutionary Jig-A-Lo chassis race cars.

Buck in the Max Simpson #41 Chevelle does battle with Doug Kenimer at Dixie (GA) Speedway in the early 1970's. (Photo from the Max Simpson collection.)

The late 1970's saw the dawn of a new era in dirt late model racing. In 1978 a Kingsport, TN. businessman, and rebel promoter known as Robert Smawley, brought dirt late model racing to the national scene with his NDRA Series. Simmons along with most of the nation's best dirt, and even some asphalt, stars came on board. The reason was simple,

Simmons powers out of a turn in a Barry White outlaw wedge race car. (Photo by Gene Lefler.)

unheard of racing purses at the time of $10,000 to win for a 100 lap event.

Buck would go on to leave his mark on the NDRA, winning the 1981 NDRA Points Title, and the '85 NDRA/Stroh's $250,000 Invitational race. He would also become the series' all time wins leader with 23 victories.

Even before the NDRA series ended in 1985 Buck was already teaming with Cowpens, South Carolina's legendary chassis builder, Barry Wright. Through the '80's and '90's the Simmons/Wright team would score almost 200 wins together. They raced dirt late models, and outlaw wedge race cars throughout the South.

The late '90's saw Simmons start racing closer to his hometown of Baldwin, GA. By this time, Simmons' beard had a little more grey, and he was carrying a few more pounds around the middle. Also, Buck's years of "hard living" had taken a toll on his health. But keep in mind this is "The

Living Legend" we are talking about here. His racing skills were clearly still there.

From the mid-'90's until 2003, he drove race cars for the likes of, Wade Hegler, Morris Partain, Shane Worley, Slab Sellers, Bruce Taylor, Tim Simmons, and finally Gerald Voyles and the John Deere green #41. Buck won his last 31 races, including his historic 1000th win, in the Voyles #41.

A few months back, I heard that a number of the younger drivers had bragged about outrunning Buck Simmons. Well I got on my facebook page, and not calling any names said, "You may have outran Simmons in the twilight of his career; when he was not in the best of health, and had to be helped into the race car." I then said, "It's a shame you didn't get a chance to race him in the prime of his career. Because you would still be standing there wondering which way he went!"

Buck Simmons racing in one of his last trips to the historic Dixie (GA) Speedway. Buck was almost impossible to beat at this track the first few years of its opening in 1969. (Photo provided by Tony Hammett.)

Buck hung up his helmet for the last time in 2003, with the last of his 1,012 wins scored at Toccoa (GA) Speedway. Sadly, on August 12, 2012, the racing world lost, in my opinion, the best dirt late model driver to ever strap into a race car. That day we lost "The Living Legend," Buck Simmons.

Here is one of my favorite photos of Buck Simmons. That old "Buck smile" never changed through the almost forty years that I knew him. It's a shame that many of today's race fans will never know just how good Simmons was behind the wheel of a dirt late model. There was simply no one better, past or present. He was truly dirt late models' "Living Legend." (Photo from the Robert Smawley collection.)

BACK OF THE BOOK PHOTOS

Jim Erp's Tri-City Aluminum race team, Larry Moore and Buck Simmons. (Photo from the Robert Smawley collection.)

The starting lineup for the 1982 NDRA Carrie Coal 100 at Atomic (TN) Speedway. That's Mike Duvall and Buck Simmons on the front row. (Photo provided by Gene Lefler.)

Buck in the #222 just after Leon Archer left the Barry Wright ride. (Photo provided by Gene Lefler.)

Simmons in the Barry Wright wedge car at Concord (NC) Speedway during a big 10 event. (Photo provided by Gene Lefler.)

Buck just after taking the win in 1985 Governor's Cup race. (Photo provided by Gene Lefler.)

Here is a smiling Simmons with the 1985 Governor's Cup trophy. (Photo provided by Gene Lefler.)

Simmons powers thru a turn at one of his favorite tracks, Cherokee (SC) Speedway. (Photo provided by Tony Hammett.)

Simmons hot lapping at Cherokee Speedway. (Photo provided by Tony Hammett.)

Buck Simmons #41 battles the #B4 of "Black" Jack Boggs at Cherokee Speedway in Gaffney, SC. (Photo provided by Tony Hammett.)

Simmons in the #41 powers by the LA Gear #00 of Freddy Smith at the Laurens (SC) Speedway. (Photo provided by Tony Hammett.)

Buck standing beside the Barry Wright #41 before an NDRA race at Concord (NC) Speedway. He would go on to win this race. (Photo provided by Gene Lefler.)

Buck taking a qualifying lap at Dixie Speedway in the Worley Monument/ Simmons Electric #41. (Photo provided by Tony Hammett.)

Buck in the Barry Wright #41 battles his former teammate, Larry Moore, during the 1982 Carrie Coal 100 at Atomic (TN) Speedway. (Photo provided by Gene Lefler.)

Buck with his daughter, Stormie Simmons, in the scoring tower at Billy Thomas' East Alabama Motor Speedway. (Photo provided by Tony Hammett.)

Here I am with Buck Simmons' daughter, Cassidy Simmons, at the 2016 "Cabin Fever" race at Boyd's Speedway. Look at that smile. It reminds you of her dad's smile. (Photo provided by Gary Parker.)

Myriad Pro and Souses on LSI 70# archival white
Type and design by Karen Paul Stone

ABOUT THE AUTHOR

Gary L. Parker, racing historian, has been around the sport of dirt late model racing for over 50 years. He has written a number of articles for such racing publications as, *Dirt Late Model Magazine*.

Bill Holder, a writer and founder of The National Dirt Late Model Hall of Fame, says Parker's first book, **RED CLAY AND DUST** is the "Holy Grail" of books on the evolution of the dirt late model.

Parker's second book, **THE ROCK-EM, SOCK-EM, TRAVELIN' SIDEWAYS DIRT SHOW**, is a history of the first national touring series for dirt late models. The National Dirt Racing Association (NDRA) was the dream of Kingsport, Tennessee's Robert Smawley, a visionary racing promoter who was clearly years ahead of his time.

HERB "TOOTLE" ESTES, is the biography of a southern auto racing legend. Estes started his career in a midget, then raced jalopies, sportsmans, modifieds, and skeeters. As NASCAR became popular during the 1950's, he drove in every division of that series, ending his career in the popular dirt late models.

BUCK SIMMONS covers the career of "The Living Legend" of dirt racing who drove jalopies, modifieds, skeeters, and dirt late models against some of the best drivers in the nation. Simmons scored 1,012 career wins and is in the National Dirt Late Model Hall of Fame.

Gary Parker is a voting member of the National Dirt Late Model Hall of Fame and is a contributor to the Georgia Racing Hall of Fame. He holds a masters degree in anthropology from Vermont College and a PhD. in anthropology from City University of Los Angeles. He lives with his wife, Elaine, in Chattanooga, Tennessee.

To order more books by Gary L. Parker

Copy this page, complete information,
and mail with check or money order
to
Gary Parker, 1517 Maxwell Road, Chattanooga, TN 37412
423-580-2690 • eparker0923@gmail.com

Name _____

Shipping address _____

City _____ State _____ Zip _____

Phone _____

E-mail (optional for shipping confirmation) _____

Red Clay and Dust
Quantity _____ book(s) @ $24.95   = $ _____

Rock-em Sock-em Travelin' Sideways Dirt Show
Quantity _____ book(s) @ $24.95   = $ _____

Herb "Tootle" Estes
Quantity _____ book(s) @ $19.95   = $ _____

Buck Simmons
Quantity _____ book(s) @ $22.95   = $ _____

Shipping first book   = $ 5.00

Shipping (quantity) _____ additional books @ $3.00   = $ _____

                                     SUB-TOTAL = $ _____

TN residents add sales tax @ .0925 x sub-total   = $ _____

                                     TOTAL = $ _____

Mail completed form with check or money order to:
Gary Parker, 1517 Maxwell Road, Chattanooga, TN 37412
423-580-2690 • eparker0923@gmail.com
or go to
www.waldenhouse.com – or –www.amazon.com

www.ingramcontent.com/pod-product-compliance
Lightning Source LLC
Chambersburg PA
CBHW042132160426
43199CB00021B/2892